GENESIS

Madame Guyon's
Commentary on the Bible

Christian Books Publishing House

Genesis

GENESIS.

WITH EXPLICATIONS AND REFLECTIONS REGARDING
THE INTERIOR LIFE.

CHAPTER I.

1. *In the beginning God created the heaven and the earth.*
2. *The earth was without form and bare, and darkness covered
   the face of the abyss. And the Spirit of God was borne
   over the waters.*

God created the heaven and the earth in the beginning, and He
created them by the Word; for it is by Him that everything
has been made, and without Him has there been nothing made:
He was at the beginning in God. This is a beautiful figure of
the regeneration or re-creation of the soul sunk in the nothingness of sin. It is from this frightful chaos that God draws the
sinner to create him anew; but He does it only by Jesus Christ.
For as from the beginning the first step towards conversion is
this new creation, and as St. John assures us that from the
beginning was the Word, and that everything has been made
by Him, and without Him has there been nothing made, it
must also be said that from the beginning of the Christian and
spiritual life, as well as in its progress and consummation, everything is wrought by Jesus Christ, who is " the Way, the Truth,
and the Life." God, then, by His Word regenerates and re-
creates this soul which was as annihilated by sin. And how
does He do this? Here is the order expressed in this first
verse of Scripture, which, relating what happened at the beginning of the ages, points out to us the conduct of God in the
conversion of the sinner, which is the first step and entrance
into the Christian way, both spiritual and interior.

In the first place, *God creates the heaven and the earth.* This
marks the two renewals that must be wrought out by penitence,
the exterior and interior; for we must quit sin not only of the

body, but also of the heart and spirit. But as outward conversion must always depend on that of within—that is to say, on that of the heart and spirit, represented by the heaven—it is here said that God created the heaven and the earth. He begins by the heart and spirit, then He reforms the outer. The first stroke of conversion is made within. God creates this spirit, drawing it out of the horrible chaos where it lay; then He frees the body from sin. He gives this heart a secret proneness to be in Him who is, and without whom it can never exist; then He leads the exterior to quit the engagements that keep the heart in death and non-being, drawing it away from the sole and sovereign Being, to place it in created nothings.

Nevertheless this *earth*, after its creation, remains *void and without form;* that is to say, deprived of all good; whatever it may be, it is only clothed with some form and appearance—and that is all. There is yet no plant, but only a great *void*, and an extreme dearth. This is the exterior state of man in his conversion. It is added that *darkness was upon the face of the abyss*—that is to say, that this spirit and heart, like a deep abyss impenetrable to all but God, are so enveloped in *darkness*, that the poor soul does not then know what to do; it sees within itself nothing but the darkness and horrors that sin has spread there; it sees out of itself but *void* and sterility; it finds itself deprived of all good, and surrounded by every evil.

Nevertheless, although this is the case, the *Spirit of God* does not cease to *move over the waters*. What are these *waters*, if not the tears of penitence, over which grace rests, and is diffused in spite of the *darkness of ignorance* (which is the remains of sin), and the frightful vacuity of all good?

3. *Now God said, Let the light be made; and the light was made.*

This bountiful Spirit, who has brooded over the waters of penitence, seeing the grief of this ignorant sinner, sends him in the midst of his darkness a ray of His light. *God said let there be light, and there was light.* A certain lustre that emanates from God Himself, and which is nothing else but a ray of His wisdom, strikes this blind spirit, who, feeling his darkness dispersing little by little, begins to comprehend that the Word of God is an efficacious word. It is speech, and it is light. For created light is the expression of the Uncreated Word, as the Uncreated Word is the source of the light communicated to the creature. This is why the Divine Word is called the splendour of the saints; for He is a word full of light, shed abroad on them. Thus God, to create all things out of nothing, has but to speak; for His speech is His Word, and His Word is His light. God speaks then in this new creature; and what is the first word He says to it? It is, *Let there be light;* and this word is no sooner spoken than *there is light;* this darkness of ignorance is changed into a light of truth, which increases little by little, as the rising sun disperses by degrees the darkness of night. This light is a light of grace, which is the light effected by Jesus Christ, and not yet Jesus Christ the Light. It is then we can say, in the highest sense, that they who were in the darkness of sin and ignorance have seen a great light, and that the sun has risen upon those who dwelt under the shadow of the death of sin.

It is easy to see that all this is done by the grace of the Redeemer, and the bounty of the Creator.

4. *God saw that the light was good; and He divided the light from the darkness.*

5. *He called the light Day, and the darkness Night: and of the evening and the morning there was made one day.*

Scripture adds, that *God saw that the light was good;* that is to say, that this light having emanated from Himself, and being mixed with no impurity of the creature, was good, and that it was working good effects in this new creature. For it is by its means that the new creature begins to discover its first cause, and to conceive the desire of returning to Him. Thus a light shed abroad in so obscure a place, discovers the place which it leaves—the ray manifesting itself, and at the same time the abode of its original.

God has no sooner shed His lights of grace upon a heart, and the heart has no sooner responded to them by its fidelity, than, seeing the good use the soul has made of them, and the goodness of this light diffused in those dark places, He begins to *divide the light from the darkness.* Until then it was a day of gloom or of luminous darkness; but now God divides His light from our darkness, so that this mixture may not spoil it. This beautiful *light* is faith, the gift of God, coming to take possession of a soul. At the beginning, only illustrations are distinguished clearly, on account of the heavy night in which the soul lies. Not that this beautiful light is clearer and more abundant in its first illustrations than afterwards, although it may be more perceptible. It is quite the contrary; but the profound darknesses of the soul cause it to be better distinguished, although it may not be so lively as afterwards.

God then divides His light from our darkness; and it is then that it becomes purer, more extended, and more eminent, although it may seem to grow dark for man; who, on account of the division that has just been made between what is God's and what is his own, perceiving nothing but his own darkness, believes himself to be in a greater obscurity. Nevertheless, he never was more enlightened nor more luminous in his highest region; but as he is exposed before God, who, like an immortal sun, sends His light unceasingly upon him, and as he renders back to God this same light with much fidelity, everything appears obscure on his side; just as we see the moon, when most exposed to the sun at the time of her conjunction, shedding so much the less light upon the earth the more she receives of it, and appearing dark when her sun regards her the most nearly and strongly; and, on the contrary, rendering so much the more light to the earth when she is in her fulness, and receiving less from the sun. It is thus also with the soul illuminated by the divine light; when the Divine Sun sheds upon it His ardent and burning rays, it is so strongly correspondent to its God, that it perceives not His brightness and splendour; whilst, when His light is smaller, and when it receives less from its sun, it is then that it diffuses more. This is the difference between distinct and perceptible knowledges (however sublime they may appear), and the general and indistinct light of faith.

It is added, however, that the *evening and the morning made but one day.* This is understood in two ways: One, that a continual alternation of light and darkness makes but one day, the day of faith, partly luminous and partly obscure; the other, that the light, commencing as the light of life, which is that of the *morning* of the interior life, and alive with brightness and splendour, and the *evening*, signifying the state of death, extinction and stripping, make *one* complete *day*, the day of faith and of the interior Christian.

> 6. *Then God said, Let the firmament be made in the midst of the waters, and let it divide the waters from the waters.*
> 7. *And God made the firmament, and divided the waters which*

were under the firmament from the waters which were above the firmament; and it was so.

8. *And God gave to the firmament the name of Heaven. And of the evening and the morning was made the second day.*

The days of penitence being passed, *God said, Let the firmament be made in the midst of the waters*—as much as to say, Let the course of these tears be now stopped, let the heart and spirit be made firm, and let these first tendernesses be separated from the waters, which, although holy, are nevertheless procured by the *sensible.* Let these *waters be divided* from those of my grace, so that they may be pure, and without mixture.

The *waters which are above the firmament* are the waters of grace, all pure, clear, and spotless, which submerge and overflow the soul in such a manner, that they purify it in an abyss of delights. Then the waters of bitterness and grief are placed under, and the superior part, represented by the region above the firmament, finds itself plunged in a torrent of delights; whilst the lower part, the earth, is inundated with the waters of bitterness and grief. And it is these two waters thus divided— the *day* of consolation and the *night* of grief—that compose the *second* spiritual *day*, which is no other than the second period of the interior Christian.

9. *And God said, Let the waters under the heaven be gathered together into one place, and let the dry appear; and it was so.*

10. *And God called the dry, Earth, and gave to the mass of waters the name of Sea; and God saw that that was good.*

These waters of bitterness and griefs which had spread over all the soul *are gathered together into one place;* they now retire to the limits marked out for them, and these limits surround the heart. Then *what is dry appears,* and the soul begins to enter into new regions which it had not yet discovered since its conversion. This is when the dry and arid is discovered, and is much more difficult to bear than the waters of bitterness. For these waters, which before covered all the earth, were still mingled with sweetness; but they are no sooner shut up in their limits than they become sea *(mer)*,—that is to say, full of bitterness *(amertume)*, and all that they covered before is reduced into dryness.

226

Chapter I.

God gave the name of Sea to this mass of waters; for, in the division made, all sweetness seems to have retired and mounted up to the superior waters, and there remains in the inferior nothing but what is bitter, which is so closely gathered into one place, that [these waters] have much more bitterness there where they are collected, than they had before in their greater extent. *This dry (land),* says Scripture, *was called Earth.* This signifies, that it is only then that man begins to enter into the knowledge of himself, and of the vileness and baseness of his origin. Now this is done by means of this great dryness and aridity, which is produced only by God withdrawing all the waters that covered it, as much the sweet and celestial waters as those of bitterness and grief; and having drawn to Himself into the supreme region of the soul the sweet waters of grace, withholding from them the power of descending upon the earth—that is to say, the lowest parts of ourselves, in which resides the *sensible*—the dry and arid must necessarily there be discovered; but this is done in a painful manner, because the waters of bitterness are there also, not to moisten and refresh as formerly, but to communicate their bitterness without any refreshment, except at certain moments when there falls a heavenly dew, which the sun of righteousness dries up almost immediately. Nevertheless this dew fortifies, sustains, and vivifies.

It is added that *God saw that this was good.* This is said of all the preceding works—not only to teach us that all the works that God does alone, or without resistance on our part, are always good, and that nothing can be spoiled in His actions but by the mingling of the proprietary creature; but more, that each state or degree in which God places the soul possesses a goodness proper and peculiar to it; and that, nevertheless, all have their times and uses very different. For when God had created the waters, and they had spread over all the earth, He said that it was good. Shortly after, however, He changes things, and still says the same, that it is good. That which was good and necessary for one time becomes useless and dangerous for another. It is good for a time that this dry and arid earth be inundated by the waters of grace; but it is very good for another time that it be deprived of them, and that these waters retire into their place, without which their sojourn upon the earth would corrupt them, and hinder the earth from bearing any fruit. We see, then, the necessity there is of allowing God to operate in souls without mixing therewith the confused and precipitate action of the creature, which generally desires to retain the waters by efforts when God wills to withdraw them ; or to dry them up of itself, before God does it, under pretext that the state is purer. Oh almighty hand of God! it is Thine to do all things by Thy Divine Word ; Thou sayest, and it is done ; Thy saying is doing, and all that Thou doest, Thou doest well.

We must then leave it to God to do ; He will do it better than we. Oh poor creatures that we are! We believe ourselves able to do what God does, and often even to do it better than He. This is why we meddle with everything, and desire always to keep everything between our hands; but we never advance in anything; on the contrary, our eagerness hinders it from working. God performs His perfect works only upon nothingness, which does not resist Him.

11. *And God said, Let the earth bring forth the green herb, yielding seed, and fruit trees bearing fruit, each according to its kind, and containing their seed within themselves upon the earth. And it was so.*

12, 13. *And God saw that that was good. And of the evening and morning was made the third day.*

When the time has arrived, the moment of the will of God, who disposes the soul, to fill it or render it void according to His eternal designs, God commands this dry and arid earth, hitherto apparently useless, to produce the *green herb*. This is its first production. This soul, in the midst of its aridity, is astonished to see communicated to it a vivifying quality, rendering it able to apply itself to good things with facility. All these plants *bear their seed within themselves*, causing them to be reproduced and multiplied to infinity. They are yet, however, young herbs, feeble actions, and little things, which nevertheless does not prevent them appearing very great to this soul, who knows nothing greater ; and who did not even expect this strange sterility to produce so great a good. When then it believes itself possessor of the greatest things, it is still more surprised to perceive, that this same Word, which has produced in it the herb, also *produces trees, leaves and fruits*, which is quite another production from that of simple herbs. These are the most heroic virtues, which bear within themselves the *seed* of an infinity of other virtues which must be communicated by its organism.

Chapter I.

Then the soul begins to discover its grandeur and nobleness, and what is proper to it—what it can aim at, and attain to. It sees this, however, only confusedly; but it is not yet shown how these things are wrought in it, nor who it is that does them. It only comprehends with its confused sight that it is God who is the author of them; but, at the same time, imagines He has done it all on account of its fidelity.

However, it will be necessary for it to comprehend afterwards two things. The first is, that it is by the Word that everything is wrought in it, and that without Him is nothing made; therefore, God employs only His Speech (*parole*), which is nothing but His Word (*verbe*) to operate all things: "*He spake and it was done.*" This was the fault of Moses at the rock of the waters of contradiction. He wished to strike the rock, and it was only necessary for him to speak; for it was given him then to act no longer by the rod of his own operations, but to act by the Word, and to perform everything in God by the same Word. The miracles of souls well advanced in God are done by speech, without any sign or figure, which does not happen to souls still in gifts—they make use of outward actions, it not being given them to act by the Word; for it is only in God himself, and in an eminent manner, that Jesus Christ is communicated and formed in us, which is called the mystic Incarnation. Now the soul can only act by the Word after It is given it in the manner already mentioned; and it is then that speech operates everything, and that saying is doing, and doing saying. But when we, by infidelity, wish to make use of the rod and signs as we did formerly, then we displease God much.

The second thing that this soul must learn is, that these operations of grace are not done by virtue of its merits, but rather with a view to our annihilation, as the divine Mary knew, when, relating the mercies of God, she said, that they had been given, *because God had regarded the low estate of his handmaiden.* He has looked upon its nothingness, and this regard has produced in it the Word, the image of the Father, who is produced in us by His looking upon our nothingness; and in regarding us thus, He begets in us His Word, which is His speech, and in communicating this Word, it is given us to act from Him with speech alone.

This state of the production of all those virtues in the soul forms the *third day*, or degree of the interior life; but what is admirable, all these virtues come into the soul and are found

229

established there without it being comprehended how it is done; for without any labour on man's part, but that of letting himself be possessed by his God, and allowing Him to operate in him, he is astonished that God does all things in him and for him, and does them each in its time, but with an order so ravishing, that this astonished soul cries, Oh, how well He does all things! It belongs to Thee, O Eternal and Uncreated Wisdom, to cause all things to be well done; for all that is not of Thee, or comes from Thee, is but lying, error, and deceit.

If this explanation is faithfully followed, there will be seen the course of the operation of God in souls by Jesus Christ from the beginning of their conversion, and the necessity there is of corresponding to it; not, as it is imagined only by a strong activity, but much more by an entire dependence on the conduct of grace, which does not leave for a moment the soul that it has taken under protection, until it has conducted it to its end. We must then allow the Spirit of God to act in us. But it seems that, on the contrary, man labours only to hinder that same Spirit from working in him; for, instead of following the Holy Spirit by the continual renouncing of ourselves and entire resignation to His will, we seem to be desirous of preceding Him by the violence of our operations, and of obliging Him not to conduct us, but to follow us; and as our own conduct is but faults and misery, we endeavour to engage this Holy Spirit of God to walk in the road that we point out, without being willing to abandon ourselves to Him, that He may conduct us into His ways. This is what happens when we unceasingly run counter to this Divine Spirit; when we vex It even, according to the words of scripture, and when, in fine, we quench It entirely. St. Paul warns us to be careful not to use It thus.

14. *God said also: Let luminaries be made in the firmament of the heaven, that they may divide the day from the night, and that they may serve for signs to mark the times and the seasons, the days and the years.*

15. *That they may shine in the heaven, and give light upon the earth. And it was so.*

16. *And God made two great lights: the greater light to rule the day, and the lesser light to rule the night: He made the stars also.*

17. *And God set them in the firmament of the heaven to give light upon the earth.*

Chapter I.

18. *And to rule over the day and over the night, and to divide the light from the darkness: and God saw that that was good.*

19. *And of the evening and the morning was made the fourth day.*

When the third day or degree of the interior is passed, God begins to produce in the soul a new state, which is the *fourth* step of the interior Christian. This is when the soul, in whom until now everything has passed as in darkness and obscurity, begins to receive the light and diverse interior illustrations. In its highest region there is nothing more but light and heat: it has a great many *distinct lights*, besides the general one, and its state is so luminous, that even in the *night*, its time of obscurity, but an obscurity conform to its degree, it continues to have light, although different from that of the *day*. The difference between the light of the day, that is to say, the most luminous state, and that of the night, is, that by the former, objects are better discerned, whilst it itself is less distinct: a great many knowledges are communicated, and many truths discovered, although the nature of the light is not so much seen, on account of its dazzling brilliancy: whilst the latter does not nearly reveal objects, but shows itself only very distinctly. This is what often deceives souls in this degree, causing them to take the day for the night and the night for the day, thus making much more of these lights of darkness than the general one, which, concealing itself, discovers, nevertheless, by its brilliancy objects as they are.

This light of the day, being the Eternal Sun, is nothing but the light of faith, which is not so satisfying on account of its general nature, although infinitely more luminous than that of the other stars. The other lights of the night are all distinct ones—visions, illustrations, everything distinguished and perceived throughout our night of ignorance. All these lights, however, come from God, and being the effects of His goodness and power, we ought to accept them with reverence and humility; but they are, nevertheless, very different from each other. We are so blind that we prefer generally the light of the night to that of the day, and whilst amusing ourselves too much discerning *the stars of the firmament*—that is to say, the distinct lights, these visions, illustrations, and ecstasies—we do not go beyond them to lose ourselves in the general light of faith;

stopping thus to distinguish objects by these faint glimmerings, which deceive us, magnify and change them, and often make them unrecognisable. Oh, strange loss is this that the soul suffers in this degree! This is one of the most important points in the spiritual life; for if the soul is not instructed as to the difference between these two lights, it stops at the latter even to death, and never enters into the open day of faith, where truth is manifested without error and deceit.

Now, the degrees of rising and setting of these lights make known the seasons of the soul—that is to say, the state in which it is—just as the sun distinguishes the times and seasons by the different stay it makes in its signs; and the same with the moon. Thus the first approach of the interior sun produces the first spring of the spiritual life, not yet the eternal spring; its advance makes summer, a state where there is nothing but light and heat; and at length it produces by its warmth fruits, which appear in autumn; but in proportion as it retraces its steps and recedes from us, it leaves us a winter so much the more grievous, as the other seasons had been agreeable; in short, the course of these heavenly luminaries, either approaching or receding, marks the seasons and states of the soul. And as the sun finds again the sign of its zodiac whence it set out, whether it approaches or leaves us, so the soul always re-finds its God, its house and birthplace, although it may experience a fearful obscurity through the retirement of the same light that had at first advanced upon it with giant strides.

God saw that it was good—that is to say, the advantage the soul derives from His divine conduct, which makes Him terminate this fourth day or degree, to cause it to pass into another. If the soul was faithful, would it not go on its way until it arrived at the seventh day, the rest of God in Himself? But, alas! our infidelity makes us stop at the first day, without going beyond; this is why we dwell all our life in a frightful chaos.

It must be observed, that at all the days and degrees it is said, *that the evening and the morning made one day.* This shows how God composes this day or step (which is distinguished from the others), of the commencement and introduction of a degree, and its consummation; and how the beginning of each degree is like a new day opening, and its consummation—a day ended, but ended only to re-commence with greater strength. Each change of day is preceded by a night, which, in terminating, gives birth to the other again. Oh admirable mystery of God's conduct with His creatures ! If we had our eyes open to the Divine light, we would discover with infinite joy that there is nothing that takes place in the natural order of creation but is found in some proportion agreeable to the order of grace in the soul. It is this that delights the illumined spirit, making it not only discover God in all creation, but even the wise conduct that He exercises on souls to draw them to Him, so that it sees nothing in nature but what expresses something that takes place within its own interior. Thus it is very true that man is a little world, in whom everything that is done in the great universe is expressed as in epitome; but the reason we do not perceive it is, that we are not wholly penetrated with the light of Truth.

> 20. *God said again, Let the waters bring forth living animals, that swim in the water, and birds that fly under heaven, over the earth.*
>
> 21. *And God created great fishes, and all the animals that live and move, which the waters brought forth, according to their kind, and all the birds according to their kind. And God saw that that was good.*
>
> 22. *And He blessed them, saying, Increase and multiply, and fill the waters of the sea, and let the birds multiply upon the earth.*
>
> 23. *And of the evening and morning was made the fifth day.*

Until now plants had appeared upon this dry and arid earth; the luminaries had been born and had risen within the soul—that is to say, as much the distinct lights as the general light of Faith, which, although indistinct in itself, yet continues to make manifest truths as they are, provided only that we do not waste our time regarding the light itself, but make use of it to view the objects discovered to us by its means; for if we should amuse ourselves with gazing upon it alone it would dazzle us, and give to the eyes of the spirit a property which, although luminous in appearance, hinders them from discovering objects in their reality, and makes them see everything affected by it. Thus it happens to all those souls who, in place of using this light of faith to discover simply what it manifests to them, desire to reflect upon it, and see into itself, and what it is, and its different effects. Then is the eye dazzled by thus acting contrary to God's designs, who gives us this light only to make us hasten to Him by the way it opens for us. This is what causes all the illusions that take place in the way of faith, which is itself so pure, so straight, and so sure, that there are never any to be feared for the souls who make use of it in the manner already mentioned. It is not the same with the other kinds of lights, which have something diverting in themselves; for as they manifest themselves only, discovering but very few objects, and that in a very limited manner, they cannot show themselves as they are, but rather according to our comprehension, which by its vivacity represents them to itself often, under its former ideas of them, although they may no longer exist, and thus they are imagined unwittingly by the reflection of the spirit. The luminaries of the night are counterfeited by artificial lights. But the light of Faith is of a nature impossible to be counterfeited, for it absorbs in its vast extent even all the other distinct lights, surpassing them all by its clearness. It is the property of faith to surpass all things, to stop at God only; and it is in that its solidity and exemption from deceit consist, if only we use it not to contemplate it alone, but to walk unceasingly by its light.

The soul until now had well experienced all these luminous graces, but its waters have not yet been alive or vivifying. Why is it said that *God created in the waters different animals, each after his kind,* and according to the quality of the waters? The reason is, that, as we have already remarked, there are two kinds of waters, sweet and bitter. The bitter are made alive; for it is only now that the soul begins to discover that there is a germ of life in the bitterness and death that have carried it away, thus causing it to love even the bitterness itself, seeing it altogether of another extent and use from the sweet waters. It is these bitter waters that produce the greatest, rarest, and most precious things upon the earth; and it is now that the soul, having perfect discernment, prefers by its own choice bitterness to the greatest sweetness.

These sweetnesses and graces, however, continue to be living and animated. They are no longer simply lights, discovering the truth of objects without giving them; but they are vivifying flowings bringing into the soul a living principle. Then it feels itself animated by a secret and profound life, which does not leave it for a moment, even in its employments; this life is no other than charity, which is already in this soul in an eminent degree, and produces in it a germ of immortality. It is this that makes the foundation of life and grace, and of the complete and intimate presence of God. This is what operates the intimate union, but not yet the essential.

Besides this, God creates in the bottom of the heart, or rather in the highest point of the spirit, birds which fly in the consecrated airs of Divinity. These birds are sublime and elevated conceptions, but they pass so quickly, and stay so short, that they leave no trace behind; and there is this difference between what is performed in faith and what takes place under the other lights: that the others can be discerned and explained, and remain distinct in the mind: We can tell them when we see them, and make them present with us, in order to relate them. It is different with the former; they pass so quickly, that they leave no trace or remains in the imagination: this is why we can neither picture them to ourselves, nor form any idea of them whatever. Nevertheless as birds, showing themselves only by their flights, remain really in the air, where they are better heard than seen; so also, souls enlightened by the light of Faith possess in themselves these knowledges, without distinguishing them otherwise than by their song—that is to say, when the necessity arises, when we must speak, or write, or otherwise make use of them—then we see that we possess those things without conceiving that we have them; just as the birds remain concealed in their habitations, and manifest themselves only by their voice.

God bids these living animals *increase and multiply.* They increase, and are multiplied to infinity, not according to the cognizance of the possessor; for they are either shut up and hid in the waters, or lost in the air, and so high up in the supreme part, that they are completely lost to sight from the lowest.

This is the beginning and consummation of the fifth state, which forms the *fifth* day or degree of the interior Christian.

24. *God said also, Let the earth bring forth living animals according to their kind, the tame animals, the reptiles, the wild beasts of the earth according to their kind. And it was so.*

25. *God made the beasts of the earth according to their kind, the tame animals, and all the reptiles, each according to its kind. And God saw that that was good.*

When the superior part has attained to the highest pinnacle of the sublimest knowledges, then the fifth day is in its consummation, and the soul seems to itself no more to adhere to the earth (for in these last days *it* has no longer been spoken of, but light, knowledge, ardours, and love). When it is thus lost in a sea of life, and in a perfect disengagement from everything material and earthly, it is greatly astonished to see being born from its earth *animals of every kind*, who crowd round its feet, and appropriate the beautiful verdures with which it is decked, to make for themselves pasture grounds. In fine, after having been the throne of God, it finds itself the footstool of animals. Oh, state very different from the others! Nevertheless, 'tis the same God, who did the first, that operates here also. Until then we do not see the use of these things; on the contrary, they appear to spoil the earth, and to detract somewhat from its beauty; it is, nevertheless, its principal ornament, and these animals are something nobler than the plants that decorate it so much, and which now serve for their nourishment. This is the state of man when it pleases God to raise him to the highest pinnacle of his perfection, robbing him for a time of the sight of the beauties He puts into him, to let him see only terrestrial and animal operations. Nevertheless these operations are both living and vivifying; it is necessary that the *earth*, the inferior part, should also produce works of *life*. But, it will be said, all these plants with which it was decked, were they not animated? 'Tis true they had a vegetable life, but they had not a sensitive one. It is this life that must be communicated to the interior soul, no longer for the evil, but for the good; for here it is given to glorify God by the sense, there being nothing in us so poor or so low but can and ought to render some glory to its God. This man, then, who for so long had been *insensible*, is quite astonished to see himself become *sensible* again; and it surprises him all the more, as he had believed himself deprived of sensation for ever. It is necessary, however, that he should become *sensible*, but his sensation will hereafter become so purified, that it will serve him, not contrary to the will of his Creator, but in accordance with it.

Thus, then, *animals of every kind are created upon this earth.* There are carnivorous *beasts* and *reptiles*. What! This imagination that previously represented only agreeable things, luminous, and divine; this spirit that was filled with such sublime knowledges, sees itself full of reptiles and unclean animals! Will it not readily say, like another St. Peter, *I have never eaten*

Chapter I.

anything that is impure or unclean, and I will not do it. But it was said to him, *What the Lord hath cleansed, call not that impure*—that is to say, that these things are good and holy, inasmuch as they have emanated from their Creator; but the only impurity that makes them unclean is within ourselves. God makes use, however, of the troubles that these things cause us, to free us from whatever impurity there is in the *sensible*, in order to spiritualise it by degrees; and He does this only by seeming to sully it. The cattle represent our outward nature, which is extremely troublesome when it is in revolt against its Creator, but becomes extremely useful when entirely subjected to Him. There is nothing in us but in the order of our creation would be very excellent, and it is only rendered hurtful by the abuse sin has made of it. These animals, coming from the hands of God, possessed nothing but what was useful and agreeable, for they were in perfect submission to man, being in the order of their creation; they have only become hurtful to him by his own revolt, which has raised them up against him; the revolt of our spirit causes that of the flesh. But God, out of His infinite goodness, uses this very rebellion of the flesh against the spirit to render subject to Him the spirit, which has no sooner entered into perfect submission to its God, than the flesh is made subject also. *God saw that this was good*, it being of infinite use to man in order to annihilate, humiliate, and destroy him.

Many will be astonished, without doubt, that I should attribute to man states and processes that happened before even his formation, but there need be no surprise if attention is paid to two things; the one is, that (as we have already observed) nothing has passed in the universal world but takes place within man in particular, so that the conduct God has exercised in this great universe, in its creation, is still observed towards man for his reformation into the order of grace; the other is, that all that took place, in the innocence of nature, before the creation of man, who corrupted it, passes within the same man, to reinstate him, by the means of grace, into an innocence abundantly restored by his Redeemer. Therefore, without doing violence to anything, we find that, as the world has had seven ages, including that of its consummation, so also man has seven ages of grace relating to the state of innocence in nature, and which, being consummated in him, render him innocent, through grace, as much as it is possible to be so in this life. We can

237

have no difficulty in believing this, since, according to St. Paul, it is not with grace as with sin, for many are dead to the truth through the sin of one; but grace and the gift of God have abounded much more unto many by the grace of one man, Jesus Christ. The redemption, then, of Jesus Christ being superabundant, has restored to man much more than sin had ravished from him. If it please God we shall explain, moreover, how this is wrought, and how there is nothing in it contrary to the common thought of the Church.

> 26. *And God said, Let us make man in our image, after our likeness: and let him have dominion over the fish of the sea, and over the birds of the heaven, and over the cattle, and over all the earth, and over every creeping thing that creepeth upon the earth.*

When man has arrived at this point, then the *image of his God* is truly renewed in him; this image that had been spoiled and disfigured by sin is found perfectly re-established. What is this image of God? It is none other than Jesus Christ, who, being the living image of His Father, delights to retrace Himself in man, and to fully express Himself there. Thence we can see the design of the creation, and also that of the redemption. God, at the creation, made all things for man, but man He made for Himself. And as He created him after all the other creatures, as *their* crown and end; so there was only God before and after man, that *he* might tend to no other conclusion than Him. Man was the end of all the rest, but he had no other end than God. *God* then *created man in His image*—that is to say, He re-traced in him His image, which is His Son and Word, impressing upon him His Spirit; and as His delights were to dwell with the children of men, and His Son being the only object of His regards, seeing that He can take pleasure in no other than Him (for if He delights in some creature, it is only by His Son), it was necessary that, before taking man into His delights, He should make him *in His image*, imprinting upon him the character of His Word, without which He could not take pleasure in him. This was, then, the end of creation, to make images of the Word in all men, in whom the Divinity would be expressed, and who might represent it, as a spotless mirror represents the object exposed to it.

But man through sin having disfigured this beautiful image,

it was the design of the redemption that God, who delights so entirely in His Word, not being able to suffer men in whom this image had once been graven to perish, and lose at the same time for ever the image of His Word and the characters of the Divinity, was willing that His Word should come to restore it. For it is the Word-God alone that can retrace Himself—none but He can do it—and it was for that He was made man; just as we see that when a mirror has lost the object it reflected, the distant object must needs approach it, without which it could never be represented. It was necessary, then, that Jesus Christ should come into man, so that man, never more losing this Divine object, should no longer lose the image and character of the Divinity. I know that the image of God is graven so deeply in man that he can never lose it, although sin may cover it, and infinitely disfigure and sully it; and it is this that causes God's sorrow for the loss of men, and which renders Him so desirous of their salvation. All that is wrought in the soul is but to discover and renew this image; and its restoration is no sooner achieved, than man is replaced in his state of innocence. It was this that made the prophet-king cry, " I will behold Thy face in justice; I shall be satisfied when Thy glory shall appear." As if he had said, " I will behold Thy face in the justice I have received of Thee, and I shall be satisfied when Thy glory shall appear in me by Thine image which Thou hast there renewed."

It must be observed that God, in creating man, made him king over all the animals, and put them all under subjection to him, so that in this universe he had dominion over all that was not God, and was ruled by Him alone; but when through sin man rebelled against his God, all the creatures that God had subjected to him rose up against him, which made him by his sin thus change not only the particular order of His creation, but the general order of this great universe—I mean in what was subject to him.

27. *So God created man in His own image, in the image of God created He him; male and female created He them.*

God created man in His own image, making him one and simple like Himself. He cannot re-enter this first state of innocence if he does not return to this first likeness in simplicity and perfect unity, which can only be performed by quitting the multiplicity of the creature and its operations, to enter again into the unity of God, which alone can render man perfectly like unto Him.

28. *He blessed them, and said to them, Increase and multiply, replenish the earth and subdue it; and have dominion over the fish of the sea, over the birds of the heaven, and over all the animals that move upon the earth.*

29. *God said again, I have given you all the herbs bearing their seeds upon the earth, and all the trees containing within themselves the seed of their kind, that they may serve you for food.*

30. *And to all the animals of the earth, to all the birds of the heaven, to everything that moves upon the earth and is living, that they may have wherewith to feed upon. And it was so.*

31. *Now God saw all the things that He had made, and they were very good. And of the evening and the morning was made the sixth day.*

God wishes this man to *increase and multiply*—that is to say, that this image of the Word *should spread over all the earth*, so that there may be no place where He may not be delighted by the sight of His image imprinted in His creatures. Before man was created, it is said that the earth was void. How was it void, since there is no place that is not filled with the immensity of God? Ah, it is void in the eyes of God when it does not yet bear these noble creatures that are the living images of His Son. He wills, then, that this image should increase and be multiplied throughout all the earth; and wherefore that, O my Great God? It is, He says, that My delights may be multiplied; for since man bears My image, and My Word has been imprinted in him, all men are to Me places of delight.

God, as it has been said, had made all things for man; therefore He gives him dominion over them. And whence comes this sovereignty of man over all the other animals? It is by virtue of the image of the Divinity within him. This image is the expression of His Word in man. Now Jesus Christ says, "All power is given Me in heaven and earth;" so man, who was His figure and living image, had all power on the earth; and his power was so much the greater as the flowing of the Word was more abundant within him.

Chapter I.

Although we lose this power through sin, as well as the image of the Word is disfigured within us by crime, nevertheless, when the image of Jesus Christ is perfectly renewed in us, He possesses complete power over us, and so great, that we will not or even can any longer resist Him—not from an absolute powerlessness, but from an impotency caused by the order re-established in us, which having taken away from our wills not only rebellion, but even repugnance to do the will of God, we find ourselves so consolidated by resignation, by the union and transformation of our own will into that of God, that no more self-will is found in us; but we will only what God wills, and the will of God is become our own.

That it is possible for this to happen in this life is incontestable, since Jesus Christ has commanded us to ask in the "Lord's Prayer" that His will be done on earth as in heaven. If we could not experience this losing of our will into God's in this life, as the blessed in heaven possess it, Jesus Christ would not have bid us ask it; for would He have bid us ask a chimera? Or would He have asked it Himself for us when He made that admirable prayer, "My Father, may they be one, as we are one"? It is certain that this perfect unity cannot exist without the total loss of all will in opposition to God. Now it is only in him who has no longer any will or resistance of his own that Jesus Christ can say in the highest sense: "All power is given Me in heaven and earth."

This is a fruit of the Redemption, that man having attained this state, through the application of the blood of Jesus Christ, resumes his right of dominion over the other creatures, of which he is the end; for he rules everything in God, thus possessing everything in himself. This is what God desires to make apparent, when saints have been seen with astonishment to command and render obedient to them the most untameable animals, and even in opposition to the nature of the elements, as when the fire served for bath and refreshment to those whose love of their God made them rather even lose their life than live out of His will, or because they could not live safely without becoming disobedient to Him, or even because they preferred death to not pleasing Him enough.

Oh grandeur!—oh power of Jesus Christ in man, and of man in Jesus Christ, how admirable you are, but how little are you known! We all bear the name of Christians, and yet we are anything but that, since we do not know even what it is to be such. Christians, bearing the most beautiful name that ever was, learn to become Christians, and ye shall learn your greatness and your nobleness; you shall enter into a just ambition to do nothing unworthy of your birth. Oh chivalrous Christians, shedding so much blood for a false point of honour! If you would comprehend what it is to be Christians, how many lives would ye not give (if you had them) to preserve this glorious quality, and to do nothing unworthy of it? But, alas! people are ignorant of the truth and spirit of the Christian religion; they stop only at the superficial, without fathoming its essential, and thus they lose advantages without end. Ah, man is created king, and he would be a king infinitely happy, if he would allow to be renewed in him the image of Jesus Christ. Yet he ever remains a slave, for he makes his royalty consist in leading himself, instead of placing it in the dependence he owes to his God, in submission to His entire will, obedience to His conduct, and, in fine, bearing with reverence all His operations, whether gratifying or crucifying; for it may now be seen, that what has led man up to so high a state, has not been his own industry, but God's goodness alone, and the faithfulness not to resist Him. All that we can do by ourselves is to resist God, and is evil (as we shall see hereafter); and man's fidelity consists in leaving God absolute master of all that he is, interiorly or exteriorly.

And God saw all the things that He had made, and they were very good, for there is nothing better for man than to see in him the image of his God; nor more glorious for God, out of Himself, than to see Himself expressed in man. It is this that causes His ardent love for man; for God delights in beholding Himself in man; and as all His delights in Himself are to contemplate Himself, thus begetting His Word; so all His pleasure out of Himself is to see His image in man, and to form there His Word. This is what St. Paul calls the formation of Jesus Christ in us.

Man, then, ought never to regard himself out of God. If he does this, it becomes the source of his disorders, and he falls into a false presumption, drawing vanity from his vileness, and becoming forgetful of his origin. But, if faithful to look on none but God, in Him he discovers with admiration his own nobleness, without fear of pride; for he sees nothing in himself out of God, but the dust of which he is formed; but in Him he sees himself God by participation; and he sees this in such a manner as to discover at the same time, that if he cease to regard himself in his Source to view himself in himself, and if he desire to attribute anything to himself, he cannot do it without usurpation ; so that out of God he would be such a frightful nothing, that he loses all desire of ever more regarding himself.   And what is strange, the sight of what he is out of God, does not serve to humble him ; on the contrary, he becomes proud in his humiliation, and, self-deluded, he attributes to himself what does not belong to him.   It is then of great consequence for man never to regard himself, but to regard solely his God, in whom he can see himself without danger.   This contemplation of his God by man, which is nothing but a simple regard, or uplifting of the face of the spirit in God, attracts God's contemplation of man ; for the more man contemplates his God, the more he is contemplated by Him.   It is the admiration of this great marvel that makes David cry out in a transport of spirit, "O God, what is man to be the object of thy regard!"

Of the states or passages of which we have just spoken, God forms the *sixth* mystic day or degree of the interior Christian; and it is here that everything is finished for man within him. It is the consummation of the works of God in man, since the end of His labours is to retrace the image of His Son.   It is now that man quits the road, to rest in the termination, and that he comes out of the mystic days to enter into the eternal and divine day.

CHAPTER II.

1. *Thus the heaven and the earth were finished, with all their ornaments.*
2. *And on the seventh day God completed the work which he had made, and he rested on the seventh day after all the works which he had made.*

It is said that *God finished his work.*   What was the fulfilment and perfection of all His works ?   It was the work of the perfect image of His Word, after which *He rests* in Himself, and causes the soul to rest in Him, where it remains hid with Jesus Christ, its divine original.

243

But Scripture adds that *God completed the work which he had made.* All these words are necessary, and well express the interior. It is not said only *His work*—seeing that all the good that is wrought in man is undoubtedly of God ; and that "no one can say Jesus is Lord, but by the Holy Spirit"-—but it is said *His work which He had made,* to show that He had made it alone. Thus also is it with the soul arrived at the state of innocence through annihilation ; God is sole operator there, acting sovereignly, without the creature resisting in anything. *And he rested on the seventh day after all the works which He had made;* by which is meant the glory, and also the repose He finds in the deified soul, which can no longer resist Him, and being one in Him, to which He has Himself led it, He has but now to rest in it, and there to take His delights.

3. *He blessed the seventh day and sanctified it, because He had rested on that day after all the works which he had created in order to make.*

God blessed and sanctified the seventh day, because on this very day He had ceased to make all His work, absorbing the soul into Himself, into His divine life, where there is nothing now but repose, although He had created this work to be made ; but having arrived at the end of its creation, which is the rest in God, there is nothing now but to remain in this Divine repose in God Himself. There, the work is finished as to the agitation that carried it to its termination; but not as to the activity of enjoyment, which is continued in the repose, and which will endure eternally.

4. *Such was the beginning of the heaven and of the earth ; and it is thus they were created in the day that the Lord God made them both.*
5. *And that He created every plant of the field before it appeared out of the earth, and every herb of the field before it grew ; for the Lord God had not yet caused it to rain upon the earth, and there was no man to till it.*
6. *But there went up a spring from the earth, and watered the whole face of the ground.*

The beginning of the heaven and of the earth—that is to say, of the two parts of man—is God ; and as his beginning, so must be his end. He must re-enter the same place whence he set out. And

Chapter II.

as in our creation everything has been performed by the Word, and nothing has been made without Him ; so also in the return of man to his end, all is wrought by Jesus Christ, and nothing can be done without Him. He takes man from the beginning of the road, and does not leave him for a moment until He has brought him with Him into God, provided that we are willing wholly to abandon ourselves to His amiable conduct.

Therefore the Holy Spirit, who delights to instruct us in everything, assures us that *God created the plants without man having laboured at their cultivation.* These plants are the virtues which increase and germinate within the soul (when it abandons itself to God) before ever it works for their acquisition ; for the desire itself of acquiring virtue, is a virtue which God puts into the soul by His goodness alone ; and we are no sooner enlightened by the true light (which is a fruit of the free gift man makes of himself to the entire will of his God) than we know that it belongs to God alone to put into the soul all the virtues.

What, then, it will be said to me, is the care of the soul, and in what consists its fidelity, if not in the acquisition of virtues? Here is the secret, my Christian brethren : the fidelity of the soul consists in submitting itself unceasingly to its God ; and as St. Peter teaches us, *" humbling ourselves under the mighty hand of God,"* who alone can work in us all manner of good ; in placing all our troubles in His hands—for He himself takes care of us ; in renouncing ourselves continually so to remove the oppositions of nature to grace, and in so doing to resign ourselves entirely to the whole will of God, so that by this renouncement and resignation, we may give place to God to act in us in entire freedom. It is in this that man's principal work with grace consists ; but for the ornament of virtues, it is God's to make it, and He does so infallibly, provided that we are faithful to coperate with His grace in these two points. And that we may not believe this grace wanting to us, it is said that God has placed a spring, representing his grace, which *rises*, so to speak, *from the earth :* for this grace is near us, always ready to flow out into our hearts. It is added that this was done before *God had caused it to rain upon the earth :* to make us admire the care that God takes of our interior when it is fully submitted to Him, and how that when some means of perfection are wanting to us by His order, there are others supplied. Thus he caused water to spring from the earth to water His plants when there fell none from heaven.

Genesis.

7. *And the Lord God formed man out of the dust of the ground and He breathed upon his countenance the spirit of life, and a man became animated and living.*

As Scripture has taught us the spiritual origin of man, which is God himself, it now desires to show us also his natural origin; therefore it teaches us of what substance he was formed, so that he may see what he is by his nature. All that is good in him is of God and belongs to Him; all that he is by himself is only vileness and baseness. Nevertheless, as there are two states in man, the one of his creation, in the natural order; the other of regeneration, in the spiritual; it is certain that, after God has formed the interior man of the dust, which is the state of his own abjection, to which he is reduced in the vileness and baseness of the clay—his origin, He out of this dust creates a new man, and then breathes into him His own *spirit*, and not a particular spirit, so that there is no other spirit than God's animating and moving him; but this is only wrought through annihilation.

8. *Now the Lord God had planted from the beginning a delightful garden into which He put the man whom He had formed.*

God forthwith places man in the *paradise of delights*. By this is meant the sweetness of the passive state of light, of love, and of the sensible presence of God, which is the greatest of all the joys that can be had in this life.

9. *The Lord God had also brought out of the ground every kind of tree, beautiful to the sight, and whose fruit was pleasant to eat, and the tree of life in the midst of the paradise, with the tree of the knowledge of good and evil.*

10. *There flowed out of this place of delights a river, which watered the paradise, and thence divided into four streams.*

In this passive state everything flourishes in the soul, and the *trees* of its faculties are found all laden with the practice of virtues, without the soul knowing how they have been produced in the earth of its heart. These *fruits are delicious*, for then the practice of virtues is very agreeable.

The tree of life is in the midst. This tree of life is God

Chapter II.

Himself, who is the source of all life, and who vivifies by the Spirit of His grace the root of the man who has the happiness to be united to Him, so that he may bear nothing but the fruits of life. *The tree of the knowledge of good and evil* is Jesus Christ, who, being the Divine Wisdom, knoweth, as saith the prophet, "to refuse the evil and choose the good," and perfectly to discern in what both consist. Men for the most part are ignorant of this discernment; they "call the evil good, and the good evil:" they call the darkness light, and the light darkness. Their error and deception come from their trusting to their own lights, in place of asking from Jesus Christ the communication of His wisdom. This tree of the knowledge of good and evil must not be wanting in the paradise where man was to live, since this knowledge was absolutely necessary for him to conduct himself well. But he was to be contented with what the Divine Wisdom had communicated to him, which was more than sufficient for his conduct, and not to carry his ambition to desire to penetrate secrets that God willed to be concealed from him, and whose curious and magnificent research served but to blind him.

The river that watered the paradise of delights, which is the interior flower-garden of our soul, is the grace that flows into the heart of the just: and this grace *is divided into four portions*, either because it takes different names, according to its different effects, although it is always the same grace in its source; or to be diffused over all the faculties and actions of man, thus these four rivers come forth from the place of delights to water the earth; which shows us, moreover, that the grace has been merited for us by Jesus Christ, and that the very graces given to Adam after his fall were accorded to him in view of Jesus Christ, and by the merit of His redemption.

11. *The first is called Pison: this is that which compasseth the whole land of Havilah, where there is gold.*

12. *And the gold of that land is excellent; there is also bdellium and the onyx stone.*

13. *The second river is called Gihon; this is that which winds through all the land of Ethiopia.*

14. *The third river is called Tigris, which goeth towards the Assyrians. And the fourth river is Euphrates.*

The first of these rivers is the first grace given us by the means of baptism; it is thence that there comes *very excellent gold,* which is pure charity, and which is there communicated to us; *bdellium* signifies hope; and the *onyx stone* faith. Now it is certain that with this first grace infused into us by baptism, the three Divine virtues are also infused. The *second* is a river that *winds about* in the earth of our soul and its faculties, and it is the augmentation of grace which increases by diverse windings, for it grows by degrees, until it has conducted us to its limit. *The third* designates the gratuitous graces given for others; thus the Tigris (Heddekel) *goes to diffuse itself over the Assyrians*—that is to say, over entire peoples. *The fourth* marks to us the final perseverance which conducts to the eternal life, and the particular effect of which is to bring us back efficaciously into our birthplace; being a grace not only sanctifying, but also of consummation.

15. *The Lord God then took the man, and placed him in the paradise of delights, to till it and keep it.*

16. *And He gave him this commandment, saying, Eat of the fruits of all the trees of the paradise.*

17. *But eat not that of the tree of the knowledge of good and evil. For in the day that thou eatest thereof, thou shalt surely die.*

After *God has put man into* this *paradise of delights,* which is the centre of his soul, and has given him His grace to overflowing, and a grace which protects him everywhere, so that he cannot fall away without a notable infidelity; after, I say, having loaded him with such great gifts, He desires him to *dress and keep the paradise.* It is in this that the soul's fidelity consists, to dress and keep what God has confided to it.

What is this *keeping,* my dear brethren? Learn it of Jesus Christ: "Watch and pray," said He, "that ye enter not into temptation; for the spirit is willing, but the flesh is weak." We must, then, keep this earth by watching, and watching on God continually; for this is the kind of watching that God desires of us, that it may be always sustained by prayer, as David said, "I will watch on thee, from early dawn; for it is in vain that we watch over the safety of our city, if the Lord keep it not Himself." But, it will be said, if I keep not watch over myself, and thus neglecting myself, I am content to wait on God alone, I shall be surprised by mine enemies. It is quite

Chapter II.

he contrary; for so soon as we forget ourselves to think only on God, the love that He bears to us makes Him take the more care over us; for He never allows Himself to be conquered in love, although He suffers Himself to be conquered by love. Are we not much better guarded by the strong and mighty Protector than by ourselves? Whatever care we may exercise watching over ourselves, it is certain that a stronger than we would disarm us, and seize upon the very things we were guarding so carefully. But if we put all our affairs into the hands of God, shall we not be able to say with the utmost confidence, like another St. Michael, " Who is mightier than God ? "

God wishes also that we *cultivate* this delicious paradise of our interior. And what is this cultivation? Our Divine Master will teach us: " Deny yourselves (says He), and take up your cross daily." To deny ourselves unceasingly in all that nature might desire contrary to God, and resign ourselves correspondingly, so as to bear equally the many crosses, pains, and difficulties that God permits to happen to us,—this is the work of man, who, aided by the abundant waters of grace, which fail him never, dwells in the order of the will of God, and arrives thus at his end.

God permits man to *taste of all* those delights represented by the *fruits*—that is to say, of all the virtues—*but He forbids him that of the knowledge of good and evil*, which is the usurpation of our own conduct to the prejudice of the reign of Jesus Christ over us. *If you taste of it*, He says, *ye shall die;* for it is thus that we seize upon what belongs to God alone, and attribute it to ourselves, regarding as a fruit of our cares what comes from His pure goodness. And as every tree that is not grafted into Jesus Christ cannot bear good fruit, so all good fruit comes necessarily from Him, in whom we are grafted, that He Himself may bring forth fruit in us. Now he who desires to conduct himself, and who would withdraw himself from the dominion of Jesus Christ, attributing to himself by his reflection the good that God does in him by Jesus Christ our Lord, seizes upon it with complacency; and it is thus that in so marvellous a state of grace we give entrance to sin, curiosity, and self-looking into the goods of God, bringing death to it.

Although it is said, *the day that thou eatest thereof thou shalt die*, the soul does not die, on that account, the very day it commits the usurpation (I mean here not the death of sin, but the state of mystic death). It does not die, I say, this very day—it would be too happy—but it is condemned to die, and it is from that time that its punishment begins: as Adam did not die immediately after he had sinned, but he was from that moment destined to death, into the labour of which he straightway entered. It is said in the text, *ye shall surely die :* which means that God is not content with a half death, nor a thousand deaths, or mortifications, but it is necessary that a real and veritable death follow, without which there is no true death, but only an image of it.

18. *And the Lord God said: It is not good that man should be alone. Let us make for him an aid like unto him.*

This can be understood of the human nature that God has desired to unite to the Divine in Jesus Christ by the person of the Word His Son. For a God cannot suffer or satisfy, and man being too feeble to merit with justice the redemption of a world, the human nature has been given as an *aid* to the Divine, so as to work most perfectly the redemption of the human race by the Man-God. It is also the figure of the union of Jesus Christ with His Church, which, like a fruitful mother, must yield Him an infinity of children as the fruit of His blood, and also as a faithful spouse, must contribute with Him to their sanctification and salvation. It is moreover the symbol of the gracious union that God makes of certain persons in this life, to perpetuate it in the Heavens, rendering them companions in destiny, in labours, and crosses, and making them act in concert, and with uniformity of grace, as much for their perfection as for the salvation of many.

19. *And the Lord God formed out of the ground every beast of the field, and every bird of the heaven, and brought them unto Adam to see what he would call them. And the name that Adam gave unto every animal was its true name.*
20. *He called every animal by its proper name, the birds of the heaven and the beasts of the earth. But for Adam there was found no aid like unto him.*
21. *And the Lord God caused a deep sleep to fall upon Adam, and while he slept, He took out one of his ribs, and put flesh in the place thereof.*

The power of Adam over all the animals in the state of inno-

Chapter II.

cence, is a proof of the submission of all the creatures to man, and of that of man to his God: as their revolt is also a mark of his own. *God brings all the animals to Adam that he may give them names* agreeable to their nature, to show that He made him king of the animals as well as of his faculties, senses, and passions, over which the innocent man ruled absolutely: but the criminal man being subject to his passions, it is the same with all the rest. Adam being the figure of Jesus Christ, it was to Him as Adam that the *animals* (representing the animal part of man and its die r ent passions) were to be rendered subject: and the *name* so suitable that He gives them, is the sure witness that it is Jesus Christ alone who can subject to Himself the passions of man, in rebellion through sin: so also the *birds of the heaven* designate the noblest parts of the soul, its faculties, and all that belongs to them: everything being re-instated in the order of its creation only through the grace of the Redeemer.

Scripture adds, that although Adam, figure of Jesus Christ, had given so fit names to the animals, and they were all subject to him as their king, the birds of the heaven as well as the beasts of the earth, *yet he had no aid like to him.* This is explained of Jesus Christ in two ways: the first that although everything had been made by Him as the Word, and without Him was there nothing made, nevertheless this Divine Word had no *aid* like unto Him: for although He was the image of His Father, and the source and origin of all creatures, He had extended His image only in the creation of man, and this image after its corruption resembled Him no longer. And even although the human nature at the time of Adam's innocence was a living image of the Word, it is certain that it had not the perfection of that of Jesus Christ. God then in saying *Let us make an aid like unto him* had in view the hypostatic union of the Word and the human nature which was an *aid like unto Him*, but so fit, that they were to work together for the salvation of the human race, which could not be wrought without their union, the greatest of all the works of God. This aid was rendered so like unto Him, that of two natures so different in themselves, as the Divine and human, there was made but one person alone in Jesus Christ.

The other manner of explaining it is of Jesus Christ and His Church. Before the birth of the Church, there was found no aid like to Jesus Christ, but after its formation there was a veritable aid to Jesus Christ and such as works with Him for the salvation of men, having with Him but one sole and only will.

Could it be more like Him, this all holy *aid*, than to ᴸ
"glorious without spot or wrinkle or any defect?"

But how was this aid formed? *God sent a sleep* to the new
Adam. This sleep came to Him on the bed of the cross; there
from His opened side came forth a daughter and spouse whose
beauty was so perfect, that she possessed nothing unworthy of
Him who was her Father, as He was also to become her Husband. The union of Jesus Christ and His Church is so close,
in order to work with one accord, and in the one same spirit
and will for the salvation of men, that whoever belongs not
to the Church cannot appertain to Jesus Christ, and none can
belong to Him that is not a child of His Church. By the bond
of this marriage, as unique as legitimate, no one is a true son of
the Church, if he is not a child of Jesus Christ: and no one is
conceived of Jesus Christ, but must be brought forth by His
Church.

Now as Jesus Christ was in the ideas of God from the creation of the world, and as all the graces that were accorded to
men since they had need of a Redeemer, were given them in
view of His merits, the Church likewise was from that time
associated with Him for the regeneration of as many children,
as were to be born from the blood of the Saviour, which in this
sense was shed from the beginning of the world, and for the
sanctification of all the chosen whom God the Father had given
to His Son as the price of his death.

22. *And the Lord God formed woman out of the rib which He
had taken from Adam, and brought her to him.*

23. *And Adam said: Behold now bone of my bones, and flesh
of my flesh: she shall be called drawn from man, for she
was taken out of man.*

24. *Therefore shall the man leave his father and mother and
cleave unto his wife, and they shall be two in one flesh.*

25. *Now Adam and his wife were then both naked, and they
were not ashamed.*

It was from the side of Jesus Christ, opened upon the cross,
and from the blood and water that flowed out, that the Church
was drawn. This union of Adam and Eve was also the figure of
the mystical marriage of the soul with Jesus Christ: it is in
the sorrows of Calvary, and not in the sweetnesses of Tabor that

it is made: and the union of the soul with its Heavenly Spouse becomes so close, that it is then that Jesus Christ says: *It is flesh of my flesh and bone of my bones.* For it becomes so much one spirit with the Word, that it finds within itself nothing now but the Word, and as it came out from Him, it finds itself united to Him without a medium, and sees itself having for spouse Him who before was its Father. This union of the soul with Jesus Christ becomes so intimate, that although wrought in the most extreme crosses and griefs, nevertheless, these pains, far from breaking the union, draw it all the closer.

It is added, that *God gave this woman to Adam:* which shows that this union can never be wrought by the creature, being a work of God alone, and not of the will of man, who has no other part therein than that of acceptation and faithfully following all the Divine movements.

What, then, is to make the soul faithful in corresponding to what the Spouse has done for it, and to enjoy the ineffable delights of the marriage of the Lamb? It must *leave its father and mother,* without which the spiritual marriage will never be consummated in it. Who is this *father* and this *mother,* if not the old Adam and the corrupt nature, which must be left absolutely? It is in quitting ourselves by renouncement, which operates the total death, that we reach the marriage of the Lamb, and we will never arrive there by any other way. Those who are all full of themselves and imagine themselves arrived at this spiritual and divine marriage, are infinitely deceived. And if Jesus Christ was obliged to leave the bosom of His Father to espouse our nature, do we believe ourselves able to espouse Him without quitting ourselves? No, it can never be.

It is also added, that *they were both naked,* to wit, Adam and his wife, and *they were not ashamed:* which shows the perfect destitution of all self-will, self-sight, of all our own turnings and windings, of all self-righteousness, which is the state of a soul that has wholly forsaken itself. These souls live in so great a forgetfulness of themselves, that they are not ashamed of their spiritual nakedness, that is to say, of the extreme poverty of spirit and of the profound abjection to which they are reduced, not being able to see it or think of it, on account of their absorption and loss in God, which is a state of transformation and may be well called a state of true innocence.

Genesis.

CHAPTER III.

4. *The serpent said to the woman, ye shall not surely die.*

5. *But God knoweth that so soon as ye shall eat of this frui your eyes will be opened, and as gods shall ye know goo and evil.*

6. *And the woman saw that the fruit of this tree was good t eat, and beautiful and pleasant to the sight. And she too of the fruit, and did eat, and gave of it to her husband who did eat of it with her.*

Self-love under the figure of the serpent, desires to show th soul the advantage there would be in going to God by anothe road than that of blind *abandon* to His conduct, without regar to self: and that if they would throw off obedience to God an the total abandon (in which they are in an entire destitutio through the loss of their will into God), they *would know* al things, would be assured of their ways, and would not di

The inferior part, represented by the *woman, looks upon th* fruit of science and knowledge, which appears to her much mo beautiful than this ignorant innocence, in which she is kept b the grandeur of her grace: she *presents it to her husband,* de noting the superior part: he accepts and tastes of it: and by s doing, he withdraws his will from that of God, throws off Hi sway, comes out of his blind *abandon,* and sins in reality.

7. *Then the eyes of both were opened, and they knew that the were naked, and they twined fig leaves together to cover themselves.*

The eyes of both were *opened* by sin: these poor delude ones fell into confusion, *and saw that they were naked,* for hav ing lost their innocence, which served for clothing to them and possessing no good of their own, since all the good tha was in them belonged to God, there remained for them only shameful nakedness, which they endeavoured to *cover,* not being able to bear it themselves, and fearing to appear before God.

8. *And they hid themselves amongst the trees of the garden from before the face of God.*

9. *The Lord God called unto Adam, and said unto him: Wher art thou?*

Chapter III.

In this they commit two notable faults: first, that after their fall they remove themselves still further from God, for they *are ashamed of themselves:* second, that they have recourse to artifice to *cover themselves,* and believe they can fully hide their nakedness by their own industry, which consists only in feeble actions of virtue, like to leaves. To go away from God after the fall, is to come out of the way of abandon to resume and commit ourselves to the human guidance. But God, whose goodness is infinite, goes to seek for them, calls them back from their wanderings, *asks them where they are,* and what has become of them.

10. *And he answered, I heard Thy voice in the Paradise, and was afraid because of my nakedness, and hid myself.*

He *fears* to appear before God, *for he is naked.* This is the false humility of those who withdraw from the *abandon* after their fall, under pretext that they are not worthy of remaining in it, or of any longer treating so familiarly with God.

11. *And the Lord said: How hast thou learned that thou art naked, unless thou hast eaten of the tree whereof I commanded thee not to eat.*

God admirably instructs these two, showing them that their shameful nakedness comes only from their disobedience, and from their having desired to penetrate His conduct, the knowledge of which is reserved for Him alone. Therefore the serpent promised them, that when they had this knowledge they would be like to God. To be desirous of knowing where God conducts us, and the secret of His designs over us, is to forestall His rights, and to do Him an injury: on the contrary, to blindly abandon ourselves to Him, is the most sure witness of love, and the true worship that renders to Him His due.

17. *God said unto Adam: Because thou hast hearkened unto the voice of thy wife, and hast eaten of the fruit of which I forbade thee to eat, the earth shall be cursed in thy work; by labour shalt thou live from it all the days of thy life.*

18. *It shall bring forth for thee thorns and thistles, and thou shalt eat of the herb of the field.*

Here is the punishment of the superior part for having followed the temptation of the inferior and self-love. These prevaricators are condemned to *labour* with many toils and *very little fruit, the earth being cursed* in their work: that is to say, that this beautiful interior field, which under God's cultivation yielded infinite fruits, scarcely produces anything more than thorns from the time it falls into the hands of Adam.

> 19. *In the sweat of thy face shalt thou eat bread until thou return into the ground from which thou wast taken. For dust thou art, and unto dust thou shalt return.*

God condemns these two parts, or souls, to many toils and pains, until through total annihilation wrought by death, rottenness and the dust, they have returned as into the state of nothingness, in which they were when God created them: then will he make new creatures of them.

> 22. *God said: Behold Adam has become like one of us, knowing good and evil. Let us beware that he put not forth his hand upon the tree of life, lest taking of its fruit, he eat thereof, and live for ever.*

This passage admirably shows how this *knowledge of good and evil*, which is that of the works of God in us, preserves the self-life of the soul, and prevents its interior death: therefore God drives Adam from the place of delights, so that *he may no longer put forth his hand upon this tree*, and that there may remain to him no knowledge that maintains his life and hinders his death; for the remedy for his evil can only be found in his death, by which, losing his proper and infected life he re enters into the divine life, which had been communicated to him by the original justice. If he did not die to himself, he could not live again in God. The trouble and concern after the fall, and which end often in despair, are the effects of a false humility. When we are so greatly afflicted and distressed after some fault, there must be a great deal of pride and self-love in us. As on the contrary, it is the fruit of a true humility to remain calm and tranquil in our abjection, after having fallen into some shortcoming even of consequence, quietly abandoning ourselves to God, to be raised again out of His mercy, submitting ourselves by a great sacrifice to all the uses it will please Him to make of it.

Chapter IV.

CHAPTER IV.

13. *Cain said unto the Lord: My iniquity is too great to be pardoned.*

14. *Thou drivest me this day from off the earth, and from Thy face shall I be hid. A fugitive and a vagabond shall I be throughout all the world, and every one that findeth me shall slay me.*

What is it to *fly from before God*, if not to withdraw from the *abandon*, to wander as a *fugitive* in all the human ways, and to go astray on the earth in the paths of vanity, after quitting the Supreme Truth, who is God alone, and the infallible attachment that held us to Him in total *abandon?* Truly, whoever strays thus from the Almighty protector, is exposed every moment to the fury of his enemies.

CHAPTER VI.

2. *And the sons of God saw the daughters of men that they were fair, and they took unto themselves wives of all that pleased them.*

3. *And God said: My spirit shall no longer dwell with man, for he is flesh, and his time shall be not more than an hundred and twenty years.*

The sons of God are the productions of His grace in souls, and which are all pure in His hands, but they are no sooner in man, than they are changed by the mingling of the creature, which rashly desires to alloy the productions of nature with those of grace, and in order to better succeed in it, it seeks in nature *whatever is most pleasing to it;* and in attributing it to grace, it gives to nature what appertains to grace, and to grace what is of nature. God, angered at the abuse that is made of His graces, withdraws them, and declares, that *His spirit will no longer dwell with man, because he has become wholly carnal and earthly:* the effect of which is that He takes from man all that belongs to Himself. Nothing now remaining to the crea-

257

ture but the operations of nature, it finds itself so hideous, that it begins to hate itself very greatly: and it would wholly despair of ever possessing the spirit of God, if there was not given to it a light, assuring it that we can come out of ourselves to enter into God: since there is a *time* for man, that is to say, a time which God shortens even, when man is left to himself, in fine, when man is man, which is well expressed by these words: *the time of man will not be more than one hundred and twenty years:* as if to say, I have set limits to his corruption. This promise leads him who desires to be faithful to his God, to yield himself up as speedily as he can be quit of himself by a continual renouncement; and it is that hope of one day being able to quit himself by a perfect renunciation, that creates all man's confidence after the sin.

> 4. *Now in those days there were giants upon the earth. For the sons of God having taken to wife the daughters of men, their children became the mightiest of the age and men of renown.*

The giants and monsters of pride come only from the mixing of the human and the divine. All the great men of renown in the world have been those who made fleshly wisdom triumph, concealed under a little spirituality. Oh the frightful monster! You will see persons puffed up and elevated like *giants* by the estimation they have of themselves, on account of their natural talents accompanied by some spiritual maxims: and who nevertheless are buried in nature, and in the secret esteem of their own conduct. They are, however, the extraordinary men, and of great reputation. But as for those who by dint of self-renunciation have become wholly annihilated, as for them I say, they are unknown: they are not even distinguished from other men. And how would they be distinguished amongst those *giants*, since they are so little, that they appear when near them only as ants, which they tread under foot with contempt, and regard often as useless things upon the earth? But, oh God, Thou "who resisteth the proud and giveth grace to the humble," Thou sheddest it abundantly on these little valleys fitted to contain it, whilst these pompous and superb mountains cannot receive a drop without allowing it to flow down upon these little ones, who acknowledge themselves so much the more unworthy of it, the more they are filled with it.

Chapter VI.

5. *And God saw that the wickedness of men was extreme upon the earth, and that all the thoughts of their hearts turned to evil continually.*

6. *And He repented to have made man upon the earth, and it grieved Him to the heart.*

7. *And He said: I will cut off from the earth man which I have created, from man even to the animals, from the reptiles even to the birds of the heaven; for it repenteth me that I have made them.*

The expression of Scripture is admirable. Can God *repent* or be susceptible of *grief?* It is to express how much He holds in horror the abuse that is made of his graces, and how much the mingling of the flesh with the spirit displeases Him. God has an extreme desire to communicate His graces to men: He has His hands always filled ready to heap them upon them: they are, as says the Spouse, "all of gold beautifully fashioned and full of hyacinths:" denoting by that, that the excess of His love makes Him distribute His graces with so much profusion, that He cannot withhold them. But, inasmuch as His liberality is great on behalf of men, so the abuse they make of His favours offends Him so much that *He is grieved at heart.* And why? for He bears all men in the depths of His heart, as He says Himself: so that the ingratitude of man and the abuse of His graces, are what wound Him most. What then does He do? He takes away from this man all that He had given him: and with the very arm by which He had conferred favours on him, He takes the avenging blade, to *exterminate* in man himself all that He had wrought there. Oh ungrateful man, it is thy pride and propriety that make of God the creator God the avenger, and oblige Him to leave nothing in thee that He does not destroy, from the greatest to the smallest things.

8. *But Noah found grace before the Lord.*

9. *Noah was a just man, and perfect amongst all those of his time, and he walked with God.*

In a whole world there is found one man alone simple and little, who *found grace in the eyes of God.* And wherefore found he this grace? The reason is given by scripture in a few words: it is, *that he was just:* and this justice prevented him from ravishing from God what belonged to Him, and from being guilty of the crimes of the other men, who were criminal, being unjust, stealing from God His property to make a miserable alliance of it with nature and corruption.

It is said also of Noah, that he was *perfect amongst all the men of his time.* Whence came this perfection? It was in his *walking* always *with God:* he abandoned himself to Him, following His conduct, remaining attached to His ways, and filled with His presence. This is what formed the perfection of Noah, and would form that of all Christians if they were truly willing to walk likewise. But the opposite of that, the forgetting of God and the passion of conducting ourselves in our own will, causes all the evils, and effects the loss of men.

13. *God said unto Noah: The end of all flesh is come before me. They have filled the whole earth with iniquity, and I will destroy them with the earth.*

As man sins upon the earth, that is to say, as he abuses the body given him, making it serve sin in place of subjecting it to the spirit, God punishes him *with the earth,* using the body itself for its proper punishment, and often punishing sin by sin itself, which happens when God by a just decree delivers man to himself, and leaves him a prey to his passions: as it is said in a Psalm: "So I gave them up unto their own hearts' lust, and they walked in their own counsels."

22. *Noah then performed all that the Lord commanded him.*

Before being received into the ark of Salvation, which is God Himself, we must have *kept all His commandments,* and obeyed all His will, not only as to exterior actions, but also as to interior purity, which can only be acquired by the observation of the law of spirit and life.

CHAPTER VII.

1. *The Lord said unto Noah: Enter into the ark, thou and all thy house; for thee have I found just before me amongst all this generation.*

Chapter VII.

Throughout a whole world there is found only one *just* man worthy *to enter into the ark*,—which is God Himself. Yet there are so many people amongst us, who believe they are in God. We must be just to enter therein, that is to say, to have usurped nothing from God, or to have restored to Him all the usurpations we had made, leaving Him in Himself, and all that belongs to Him, to remain in our nothingness. This then is the justice we must have in order to be received into God by a most intimate union.

12. *The rain fell upon the earth for forty days and forty nights.*

20. *The water rose fifteen cubits higher than the summit of the mountains which it had gained.*

21. *All flesh that moved upon the earth was consumed by it, the birds, the animals, every beast, every reptile that creepeth upon the earth, and every man.*

22. *And every thing that lived, and breathed upon the earth, died.*

23. *There remained but Noah alone, and they that were with him in the ark.*

This is a beautiful figure of what takes place in the interior state, in which *everything* human and natural, whatever it be, must be entirely *submerged and drowned in the waters* of bitterness and grief, so that Noah, representing here the root of the soul, may remain *saved alone*, and may pass into God Himself. But it is necessary that these waters *rise above the highest mountains*, that is to say, that the faculties of the soul may be submerged by them. But if this state is grievous and afflicting for him who experiences it, consolation ought to be had in one thing, which is, that sin is drowned with the sinner, and *that there remains now only the just alone*, which is no other than man pre-eminently justified by his loss and annihilation.

The deluge marks also the passions and tumult of the age. All are submerged therein with the exception of those who are in God as in an ark, where they live in safety. There are few of these latter, although they may be of every sort, that is to say, of every sex, age, and condition.

We know that the ark is also the figure of the Church.

CHAPTER VIII.

1. *And God remembered Noah, and every beast, and all the cattle that were with him in the ark, and caused a wind to blow over the earth, and the waters began to recede.*

2. *The fountains of the deep and the cataracts of heaven were closed up, and the rains that fell from heaven were stopped.*

3. *And the waters flowed over the earth from one side to the other, and began to decrease after one hundred and fifty days.*

4. *And on the twenty-seventh day of the seventh month, the ark rested upon the mountains of Armenia.*

God remembers this root and centre of the soul which He had preserved alone, and unknown, amidst so strange an inundation. How comes it that Scripture makes mention here only of Noah and the beasts, and does not speak of his family? It was because all Noah's family was included in himself, and everything is saved in him : so likewise the noblest productions of the soul are saved by means of the centre. By the losing of the centre of the soul into God Himself, are lost there also all its operations, and its faculties, which seem cut short and altogether swallowed up, so much so that they lose their functions : but it is only for their salvation that God causes their loss in this manner ; and He saves them only on account of the soul : therefore no distinction is made for them.

God remembers also *all the beasts:* that is to say, all that belongs to the inferior part, so as to rescue it from oppression and ruin.

It is then that *this overflowing of the waters is stopped.* It is not now the inundation of the waters of grace : they are the waters of wrath and indignation, and the torrents of vengeance, that have overflowed. But, oh Goodness of my God! Thou willest only the loss of the criminal : Thou willest only the extinction of sin in its root and branches : and Thou overwhelmest it thus only to preserve the just in true justice : that is, this beautiful portion of Divinity distributed in the soul, almost disfigured by its corrupt nature and the sin that surrounded it. The deluge is only to drown what is bad in this corrupted nature, but God preserves whatever is good, which comes immediately from Himself, and is represented by the beasts saved in the ark.

Chapter VIII.

But how does God stay this deluge, and what means does He take for this? He sends a living and vivifying *breath* of His Spirit, which dries up the waters of iniquity and gives life again, according to this beautiful passage, "Thou sendest forth, O Lord, Thy Spirit, they are created: and Thou renewest the face of the earth."

When this wind of Salvation begins to blow upon the soul, it *agitates* it at first in such a manner that it cannot at all discern whether it blows for its salvation or its ruin : when suddenly it is astonished to see *that the ark rests upon the mountains of Armenia.* That is to say, that peace and tranquility begin to appear upon the highest point and part of the spirit, where God discovers Himself by a little ray of His wisdom, making this soul comprehend that its loss is not without resource, and that there is some hope of salvation for it.

6. *And after forty days Noah opened the window of the ark, which he had made, and sent forth a raven,*

7. *Which went forth to and fro, until the waters were dried up off the earth.*

The raven signifies the proprietary soul full of its own will, which stops at everything it meets : everything forms a rest for it, but a deceiving rest, for it immediately finds unstableness there.

8. *He sent also a dove after the raven to see if the waters had ceased to cover the earth.*

9. *But the dove found no rest for the sole of her foot, for the waters covered the whole earth; and Noah put forth his hand and took her and brought her back into the ark.*

But the *dove* represents the abandoned soul, already lost and transformed in God, which comes forth from Him to act abroad if such is His will; I mean, that it comes out of its mystic repose, when Noah, in this place representing God, sends it abroad for the good of the neighbour : however, as there is nothing for it upon the earth, it finds no rest for its feet, that is to say, upon which it can lean: therefore, without stopping at anything, it returns into the mystic repose, where the Divine Noah, putting forth His hand, receives it into Himself.

This represents the annihilated state, in which the soul finds nothing more for it upon the earth.

> 10. *And he stayed yet other seven days: and again he sent forth the dove out of the ark.*

Seven days afterwards, representing the years of the perfect annihilation, it is *put forth again out of the ark:* and then it everywhere finds its resting place, as in the ark itself, all the world having become God for it: then it rests everywhere without stopping in any one place: and this is now the Apostolic life.

> 11. *And she returned unto him in the evening, bearing in her mouth an olive branch, whose leaves were green: so Noah knew that the waters were abated from off the earth.*

It bears everywhere the sign of peace, but without retaining anything of it for itself: it *carries it to* the Divine *Noah.* This soul in the Apostolic life takes nothing to itself of what it does for God: but with an admirable fidelity, it *brings* back to Him the *olive branch:* and it is then that it, and all its like, who were also shut up and confined in the ark, can come forth from it in all safety, and have no more need or means of protecting themselves from the deluge. They are no more straightened or sustained by anything created, and everything is salvation for them without any assurance of it. It is on this account that it is known that *the waters are abated from off the earth:* and that there is nothing more to be feared for these souls upon the earth, unless that by some dangerous turning back to themselves, they should give entrance to infidelity, which is, however, difficult in this degree.

> 15. *Then God spake unto Noah and said unto him,*
> 16. *Come out of the ark, thou and thy wife, thy sons, and thy sons' wives.*

This represents the care that God takes of souls that are abandoned to Him, and who think only of living in repose in the ark of perfect resignation. He warns them of everything in its time. This is why the care that Noah took of sending out the dove would appear useless and offensive to Providence, if it were not so mysterious as it is. Learn, oh souls, who are in the ark of God by His order, that is to say, in the mystic repose, that we must not come forth from it, for the practices of the Apostolic life, except by the same order of God, which He will point out to us every moment by His providence.

20. *Now Noah built an altar unto the Lord, and took of every animal and of every clean bird, and offered unto Him a burnt offering upon that altar.*

21. *And the Lord smelled a sweet savour, and said: I will no longer curse the ground for man's sake.*

It is then that the sacrifices of the soul have a *sweet smelling savour* for God; there is nothing more unclean or impure in them. Whilst the soul is in the ark, that is to say, in the divine repose preceding the permanent Apostolic life, it *offers* no *sacrifices*, everything having ceased with it. But from the time it is set at full liberty, it then *offers sacrifices*, whose odour is a sweet smelling savour to God: which had not been until then: for it is not said before this that the sacrifices had been of a good odour before God. Now the odour of this sacrifice is so agreeable to Him, on account of its purity and simplicity, that He is constrained to swear that He *will not any longer curse the ground:* the little faults of this soul, says God, will not any longer be disagreeable : for it is innocent, and there is no more malignity in it: there remains only to it the feebleness of its origin : I will not again take away from it this life, for it is not corrupted like the first, and it exists in me.

CHAPTER IX.

1. *And God blessed Noah and his sons, and said unto them, Be fruitful, and multiply, and replenish the earth.*

It is then that we *multiply upon the earth* by the souls that we win to Jesus Christ, to justice, and to the interior.

2. *I have brought into your hands every animal, everything that creepeth upon the earth, and every fish of the sea.*

3. *Every moving thing that liveth shall be meat for you.*

Man is re-established in a state of innocence after the afflictions of the deluge, and enjoys the advantages of it, shown by the *power* he receives over *all the animals*, and the freedom of *eating of everything.*

4. *Only of the flesh with the blood thereof shall ye not eat.*

Nevertheless there is given him a new commandment: no longer to eat not of the fruit of knowledge, or of flesh: but only *not to eat the flesh with the blood,* nor the blood separately. This division of the flesh from the blood marks the separation of the spirit from sense, which must never be united again, except in the perfect order of God, after their purification.

9. *I will establish my covenant with you, and with your seed after you.*

Then God makes a covenant with man, by the most intimate union, transforming him into Himself. This is the spiritual marriage, and cannot any more be broken.

Therefore God gives a token and sign of this covenant, and sets it in the heaven: that is to say, He renders this soul so immovable, and so strong over everything, that it can no more fear the deluge: for its transformation renders it as stable as the heaven itself is invariable, and keeps it covered from every attack.

12. *God said, This is the token of the covenant that I will establish with you, to endure for perpetual generations.*

This is the immovability, and *permanent* state of a soul, in union and transformation.

13. *I will put my bow in the clouds to be the token of the covenant which I have made with the earth.*

14. *And when I bring clouds upon the earth, then will my bow appear in the clouds.*

Though the soul be *covered with the clouds* of outward afflictions, *this sign* of thorough immovability will not cease to appear: on the contrary, it will be in the clouds themselves that it will be most remarked: thus the rainbow appears only in the cloud. This is the infallible mark of the transformed state : all those who have not yet attained to it, experiencing from time to time vicissitudes, and their immovability being not yet permanent for ever.

> 20. *And Noah was an husbandman, and began to till the ground, and planted the vine.*

Noah is the figure of our Lord Jesus Christ, who comes once more to *cultivate* our *earth*, which was become wild again through sin, and submerged by the waters of the deluge: barren as it was, He now renders it fruitful : He gives facility to the exterior to employ itself in every kind of good. But how does He cultivate it, and what does He plant there ? *The vine*—the figure of charity. Jesus Christ coming into the soul that has arrived in God through the loss of everything, and incarnating Himself in a mystical manner, *plants there the vine*, that is to say, in the sense of the Spouse, He there ordains charity. Now, as grapes have the property of giving everything to others, without retaining anything to themselves, so perfect charity empties the man who is filled with it, and does not allow him to possess anything that he does not distribute.

> 21. *And he drank of the wine, and was drunken : and he appeared naked within his tent.*

As Jesus Christ comes into the soul only to render it a participant in His states, He causes it to bear them all in a marvellous order. Jesus Christ *drank of the wine* : He drank it in the cup, and was drunken. This is understood in two ways : firstly, of the shame that He bore, as saith the Prophet, " even to being filled full of it : " secondly, of the wine of the wrath of God, which was poured forth upon him for the sins of men. It was from this dreadful cup that he asked his Father to exempt him ; " Let this cup pass from me," said he : "nevertheless let Thy will be done."

He looked upon His passion in two ways, or rather, He separated two liquors in His cup. The first was that of the shame and sufferings : and it was this that He desired to be filled full of : as He witnessed to His disciples, "that He had a great desire to eat the Passover with them before suffering." In this Passover He drank this first cup, and was so drunken, that from that moment He thought of nothing else than anticipating the torments. The other cup wsa that of the garden, and was the wrath of God upon the sins of men. Oh this was so fearful, that after drinking it, He changed this wine into blood, and sweated the blood over His whole body, as if to say, O Eternal Father, just God and avenger of a crime which merits still more chastisement and indignation than what Thou makest to appear! I drink all Thy wrath, and change it into my blood, so that my blood may assuage it on behalf of men! Let the first cup, which is that of suffering, pass to my chosen and well beloved ones: for it is only of that I say to them: "Drink of it all of ye and be drunken, my friends." But as for the cup of Thy fury, let it terminate in me, or rather, let it pass beyond, and let it go everywhere to exterminate sin, sparing the sinner."

When Jesus Christ comes into a soul truly annihilated, and no longer living in itself, but in whom He alone lives, He completes in it what was wanting in His passion, that is to say, He makes in it an extension of this same passion, and generally He intoxicates it with His first cup : but He reserves the last for the chosen souls, and He makes them drink it at two different times: one is, when He exterminates their proprieties and annihilates them ; it is then that such a soul experiences nothing more in itself but the wrath and indignation of God. The other time is when it has become another Jesus Christ ; oh, then it drains this cup of fury for the sins of others like Jesus Christ : but with so much horror, for God, whilst His indignation lasts, conceals from it that this is for others, and only discovers it to it afterwards, or at the most, in asking its consent. For God usually asks the consent of the soul, before making it suffer for the neighbour; and it is then that the soul is moved to sacrifice itself to the justice of God, and to all His will.

The *nakedness*, in which Noah appeared in his drunkenness, marks the state of nakedness in which the souls must remain that are intoxicated by afflictions, shame, and ignominy, as well as those who drink the cup of the wrath of God. He holds them in such an entire stripping of all the sensible and perceptible graces, of all the gifts and communications, that served them as a garment to hide what might cause them confusion, that at last they often appear in their own eyes and those of others, shamefully naked. There is seen in those persons nothing now but feebleness and impotency : being stripped by the power of God, all their miseries, which were concealed under the abundance of graces, are discovered : in fine they appear to the eyes of the creature in a most abject state. This is the state of Jesus Christ himself upon Calvary, who, not content with being intoxicated with shame and ignominy, was willing to be *naked:* and this exterior nakedness, shameful in appearance, was only the figure of the stripping of his soul, which was so great, that he even cried: "My God, my God, why hast Thou forsaken me?" Thou who art my only sustenance, why hast Thou abandoned me? As he is the example of the stripping of souls in the state of sacrifice in which He keeps them, He must also be their only consolation.

22. *And Ham, the father of Canaan, saw the nakedness of his father, and told his two brethren without.*

23. *But Shem and Japhet stretched a garment upon their shoulders, and went backwards and covered their father's nakedness.*

There are two classes of persons who *see* these souls in their *nakedness.* Some like Ham laugh at them, murmur against them, and take occasion thereby to decry the Spirit of God, seeing these persons now so feeble after having been so strong. Others, on the contrary, *covering them with the mantle of their charity*, excusing their faults, and regarding them in their source, as a stripping caused by the abundance of the wine of bitterness, grief, and shame, with which they have been intoxicated, consider that as an effect of the goodness of God, who is destroying in them sin and all its appendages, in order to dwell there alone: and these receive the blessing of God, whilst the former are punished for their temerity. We must excuse all that is excusable, and lean rather to the side of mercy than to that of severity.

CHAPTER XI.

1. *All the earth at that time was of one speech and one language.*

This is the uniformity of the souls who have come out of the deluge, who truly all speak but one language, being all taught of God: and who have but one speech, since it is the same Spirit that speaketh in them.

269

4. *They said, Let us build to ourselves a city and a tower whose top will reach heaven; and let us make to ourselves a name before we be scattered over all the earth.*

This is the picture of souls who aspire to be holy by their own works, and believe themselves able to succeed in it by their natural efforts, without perceiving their mistake. These subtlely presumptuous people amass together, and pile up practice upon practice, in order, say they, to render ourselves holy. They look for everything from their own efforts: and without considering what they are doing, they think to give law to God. Therefore Scripture says, they built of bricks and slime, showing by that, that it was all of the invention of man.

5. *Now the Lord came down to see the city and tower which the children of Adam built.*

God lowers Himself to *see* their temerity, the vanity of their works, and the productions of their caprices; because He Himself did not build.

7. *And He said: Come then, let us go down into this place, and let us there confound their language, that they may no longer understand each other.*

They change their language, because that having withdrawn from simplicity in action, they also withdraw themselves from simplicity in discourse, and God suffers them to lose this first language of innocence, which was no longer conformable to their works. This was then the beginning of trouble and confusion. Acting in the selfhood produces all the trouble and confusion of the interior. Men having lost the language of God, which is simple and unique, have all a different one.

8. *So the Lord scattered them abroad from this place over the face of the earth; and they left off building the city.*

9. *Therefore was this city called Babel; that is to say, Confusion.*

From that time they are no more united. *The Lord scatters them:* and most frequently they are constrained to *leave* everything, not being able to make any progress, nor to make themselves understood by others, nor to hear God. God recedes from them, and *scatters* them on account of their interior *confusion*, caused by their proprietary practices. The ark, constructed by the order of God, was the abode of peace : *Babel*, built by men, was the habitation of trouble and *confusion*.

29. *Abram's wife was called Sarai.*
30. *She was barren, and had no children.*

Sarai is barren in her own country : likewise the soul that is still in itself, cannot be fruitful.

CHAPTER XII.

1. *The Lord said unto Abram, Get thee out of thy country, and from thy kindred, and from thy father's house, and come into a land that I will show thee.*

This is the figure of the calling of the soul to *come out* from itself. God *speaks to it* in the depths of the heart, and instructs it that there is another *land* than that which it inhabits : and that if it is faithful to follow Him by total *abandon*, He will show it to it, and introduce it therein.

2. *Out of thee will I bring a great people : I will bless thee, and make thy name great, and thou shalt be blessed.*

God promises moreover to this soul, that when it shall have arrived at this land, which is the repose in God, it will possess a *great nation*, and will be *glorified.* He only asks of it for all this that it abandon itself to Him by the renouncement of itself, and that it allow itself to be conducted to Him in an entire destitution.

3. *And I will bless them that bless thee, and curse them that curse thee : and in thee shall all families of the earth be blessed.*

Who will not admire how much God is concerned about the souls who abandon themselves to Him, how He Himself takes

271

in hand their defence, how that on their account He shows mercy to so many people, and the *blessings* that they draw down upon all the persons united to them! This is so real and so true, that those who have experienced it will be ravished to see it so well pointed out under these figures, and will be charmed to see the wholly natural order in which all these things are expressed even in the ancient Scripture.

4. *So Abram departed, as the Lord had commanded him.*

Such a strict obedience as this of Abram's marks the fidelity and promptitude with which the soul ought to *come forth* from itself to follow God.

7. *The Lord appeared unto Abram, and said to him, Unto thy seed will I give this land.*

God's promises are always infallible, although they may not be performed according to the conception of him to whom they are made. Those persons who, at the beginning and during the way, have interior words or promises, ought not to stop at them, nor give their judgment on them, nor make any interpretation of them. The truth of these words is in God, and they are only rendered true for us in their accomplishment, which is very often altogether contrary to our expectation.

7. *Abram built an altar unto the Lord, who had appeared unto him.*

8. *And he passed from thence towards the mountain on the east of Bethel, and pitched his tent there, having Bethel on the west; and Hai on the east; and in this place he again built an altar unto the Lord, and called upon his name.*

9. *Abram journeyed still further, advancing towards the south.*

This *altar* which *Abram built to the Lord in the place where He had appeared to him,* instructs us that we must always offer to God sacrifices of all the graces He imparts to us, and in the very place that He gives them, receiving them only to send them back with fidelity to their origin. There are few souls who act like Abram: every one appropriates the graces of God, and retains them in Himself. This goes even so far, that we are often afflicted when He withdraws them; we complain of it to ourselves as if He were robbing us of something of our own.

Chapter XII.

Nevertheless He only takes what belongs to Him : if we were not proprietary, although God should withdraw His favours, we would not even pay attention to it : and as we would not stop at them on their reception, but on the contrary go beyond them all, we would thus, without reflection, suffer them to be taken back again to Him who gave them. Yet we see nothing but persons lamenting over the abstraction of consolations and sensible graces, and making this pass for great interior pains ; when, nevertheless, it is no other thing than great *propriety*.

You will tell me, without doubt, that you are not afflicted at the privation of these gifts, but that what grieves you is that you fear to have given cause for this by your infidelities. Oh deceit of nature, how well you conceal yourself under pretexts ! If, my brethren, it is the fear of our infidelities that afflicts us, let us humble ourselves for these very infidelities which have given cause to God to act thus, and at the same time, let us be delighted that He should deprive us of His goods, and that He should not bestow them on us, for fear we may abuse them : we ought also to have a holy joy that He does justice to Himself. This then is the disposition of the truly humble soul ; far then from bewailing and being alarmed at these privations, and continually tiring the directors with them, we ought to be humbly joyful at these abstractions, and never desire anything other than what we possess.

It is also said that *Abram built an altar in another place :* to show that he went from sacrifice to sacrifice ; and it is added, that he *journeyed still further towards the south*—to show that he went beyond all things to go to God alone.

10. *And there came a great famine over that land.*

The abandoned soul must, like Abram, remain faithful—not to be at all astonished at the aridities, and seeing only afflictions and crosses in a road, in which God seemed to promise nothing but sweetnesses ; it must follow God indefatigably through all its bitternesses, without ever stopping or being discouraged.

11. *Abram said to Sarai his wife,*
13. *Say, I pray thee, that thou art my sister, that they may treat me well on account of thee, and that my life may be saved on thy behalf.*

This apparent fault of Abram, by which he seems to dissimulate somewhat, and to expose the honour of his wife to preserve his own life, teaches us by the use that God makes of it, the care that He Himself takes of correcting the faults and wanderings which fear and weakness cause those souls to commit, when they do not come out of the *abandon*, and do not quit the way He taught them since they gave themselves to Him. This Divine conduct over Abram, and this permission appear so admirable to those who are in the light of truth, that an infinity of volumes would be necessary for its full explanation.

17. *And the Lord plagued Pharaoh and his house with great plagues because of Sarai, Abram's wife.*

God *punishes Pharaoh* for an innocent fault, which, according to appearance, was more in Abram than in him; and He recompenses Abram for a shortcoming apparently real. Who will penetrate the secret judgments of God? But who can sufficiently admire the surety of the *abandon* when everything seems most desperate? Oh! God saves both the life of Abram and the honour of his wife, on account of the faith of this patriarch who had fully abandoned them to Him.

CHAPTER XIII.

1. *And Abram went up out of Egypt, he, and his wife, and all that he had, and Lot with him, into the south.*

2. *And Abram was very rich, and possessed much silver and gold.*

3. *And he returned by the same road that he had gone, from the south even to Bethel, unto the place where he had pitched his tent, at the beginning, between Bethel and Hai,*

4. *Where the altar was which he had built, and he there called upon the name of the Lord.*

There is nothing in Scripture that has not an admirable signification. It is said that *Abram went towards the south;* this is, as we have explained, that he always went to God: and yet it is added, that he *returned by the same road, and came from*

Chapter XIII.

the south even to Bethel. What does this signify? There appears a contradiction; yet there is none. The reason is that all the roads lead to God. He who stops at none, and makes use of everything he meets, and all that happens to him to hasten to God with eagerness, finds Him assuredly.

It is added also, that he possessed a *great deal of riches;* but he brought them to the place of the *altar,* that is to say, that he sacrificed them all to God, and that he advanced equally towards Him by whatever road there was, whether he was conducted by prosperity or by adversity; everything was for him *one road* to proceed to God and to *call on His name.*

6. *The land was not sufficient to bear them together, for their riches were very great, and they could not dwell together.*

7. *Wherefore there arose a strife between the herdsmen of Abram and those of Lot.*

Too abundant interior *riches lessen peace* and union between the servants, who are the passions. These cling to them and lean upon them: and tasting them naturally, imperfect zeal arises.

8. *Abram then said to Lot, Let there be no strife, I pray thee, between thee and me, nor between thy herdsmen and mine, for we are brethren.*

9. *The whole land is before thee. Separate thyself, I pray thee, from me; if thou goest to the left, I will go to the right, and if thou choose the right, I will take the left.*

10. *And Lot lifted up his eyes and beheld all the country along Jordan, which, before God destroyed Sodom and Gomorrah, appeared a goodly land, well watered even as a Paradise of delights.*

Abram, who had peace in himself and peace with his God, could not bear *strife between his herdsmen and those of* his kinsman, and above all for the goods which he held from God alone, and to which he was so little attached that he was ready to sacrifice them a thousand and a thousand times. His *abandon* and indifference were so great, that he *gave the choice of country to* his nephew, although the preference was due to him. *Lot,* being very far distant from this faith and *abandon* and disengagement of Abram, *chose for himself the most delightful place.*

How many of these persons are there who seek in the service of God the delights of the spirit, in place of seeking there only death, renouncement, the cross, and bitterness! The issue will well show how much more advantageous it was for Abram to abandon himself to God, than for Lot to choose.

11. *The two brothers separated from each other.*

God is not content with drawing the soul out of itself: He *separates it* also from everything that could retard it, however good it may be; thus Abram might have been hindered in the way of God by the affection that he entertained for Lot, or might have been in danger of taking some natural satisfaction in his company.

14. *The Lord said unto Abram, after Lot had departed from him, Lift up thine eyes and look from the place where thou art, to the north, to the south, and to the east, and to the west.*

15. *For all the land which thou seest, to thee will I give it, and to thy seed for ever.*

Oh excessive goodness of God—recompensing a soul so soon as it leaves itself in something out of love for Thee! With what tenderness does He speak to Abram *after he had separated himself from Lot!* A good thing which serves us for support and company, hinders the communication of God, and stops the course of His graces. These promises, reiterated to Abram, were only performed according to the letter four hundred years after they were made, and after bloody battles between the people of God and their enemies; to instruct us to give neither sense, nor time, nor manner, nor anything determinate to the interior words spoken in the hearts of the servants of God.

16. *I will multiply thy seed as the dust of the earth; so that if a man can number the dust of the earth, so shall thy seed be numbered.*

17. *Arise, walk through the land in the length of it and in the breadth of it: for I will give it unto thee.*

God is admirable in His rewards, even temporal ones: He measures these, as well as the eternal, according to the nature of the renouncements made out of love to Him. Abram has no sooner separated himself from his nephew to do God's will, than God promises him, as the price of the sacrifice of one single man, the most numerous race that ever was.   This great nation was promised him for this first renouncement, as the sacrifice that he made of Isaac merited his having Jesus Christ in his posterity.   When we separate ourselves from the creatures for the love of God, whether from friends according to the flesh, or even from imperfect spiritual ones, God gives us for that an inconceivable number of friends of another kind, who are our friends in Him and for Him.   For the children and nephews that we have abandoned for His love, He gives us an innumerable mnltitude of spiritual children; as it is promised in Isaiah, "Sing, O Barren, thou that didst not bear, for more are the children of the desolate than the children of the married wife."

The earth that *God promised* then to Abram was not only the material earth that he saw, but it was also the earth of his heart, which is the reward promised to the meek.   It is as if God had said to him: Immediately that thy heart is disengaged from everything that conld attach it to the earth, it will possess itself in perfect freedom, which will have no more limits than thine eyes can have in this land which I destine for thee ; and as thou canst not see anything here which does not belong to thee, so likewise art thou master of all things by the fidelity of thy renouncement.

CHAPTER XIV.

11, 12. *The conquerors, having taken the spoil, took Lot, Abram's brother's son, who dwelt in Sodom, with all that he possessed.*

16. *And Abram brought back with him all the spoil that they had taken, and Lot his brother, with all that he possessed, the women, and all the people.*

Abram is rewarded for having separated himself from Lot, and Lot is punished for having parted from Abram.   Souls who leave all for God, receive from Him new favours with the highest peace and tranquillity.   But they who, through interest or distrust, separate themselves from the just, have for their lot only war, trouble, and chastisement. Lot represents those who separate themselves from the souls of faith and *abandon*, to live in assurance in the strong city of reason and leaning upon the creature, where, nevertheless, they find themselves still more in danger : as much on account of the instability of the creatures, who cannot sustain them, as that God justly abandons them to themselves on account of their presumption.

The *help* so opportune that *Abram renders to his nephew*, marks the care that the abandoned souls take of those even who separate from them, and how they yet continue to succour them in time of need.

18. *And Melchizedek, King of Salem, offered bread and wine, for he was priest of the Most High.*

19. *And he blessed Abram, saying, Blessed be Abram of the most high God who has made heaven and earth.*

It belongs to the only *Melchizedek, priest* of the *living God*, to *bless Abram :* for He alone knows and approves the pure and sublime way of the *abandon*. This is representative of the true priest, who gives to the soul a double refection after the combat, namely, of the word of life, and the holy eucharist.

20. *Abram gave to Melchizedek the tenth part of all he had taken.*

This soul of faith, seeing that he who is given as a guide for it is the priest of the Lord, submits to him, and recognises him as such, and gives him the tithe of all it possesses, which is, to obey him, for the love of God, and as God Himself.

22. *Abram said to the King of Sodom, I swear by the most high God, possessor of heaven and earth,*

23. *That I will take nothing of all that is thine, from a thread to a shoe latchet, lest thou shouldest say that thou hast made Abram rich.*

This is the generosity of abandoned souls who walk in the way of faith, to *refuse all riches* and all the supports of the faculties, only to have God alone. They reject all the rest, and raising themselves by a holy boldness, even to the heaven, they find nothing worthy of themselves out of God, who, as their only treasure, enriches them with Himself.

CHAPTER XV.

1. *After these things the word of the Lord came unto Abram in a vision, saying, Fear not, Abram: I am thy protector and thy exceeding great reward.*

Man could not give God a stronger proof of his love than in despising everything else to content himself with Him alone ; therefore God hastens to witness to him His complacency by words of the extremest tenderness, assuring him that He is his protector, and that He Himself will be *his reward.* Oh inconceivable happiness—God Himself will be the compensation for these little things which we quit for Him ! Truly, oh Paul, there is no comparison between the ills of this life and the glory which shall be revealed in us ; for what could enter into comparison with the possession of a God ?

2. *And Abram answered : Lord God, what wilt Thou give me ? I shall die childless,*
3. *And the son of my servant will be my heir.*

This faithful servant seeing himself near his end without having received the fulfilment of the divine promises, and continuing to abandon himself, seeks nevertheless some means of being assured of the future, which is designated by the *heritage;* and he thinks of taking measures himself.

4. *The Lord said unto him, This shall not be thine heir, but he that shall be born of thee shall be thine heir.*
5. *And He brought him forth abroad, and said, Look now towards heaven, and tell the stars, if thou be able to number them : and he said unto him, So shall thy seed be.*

God, whose goodness is infinite, quickly proceeds to frustrate all the measures that Abram's weakness had made him take, by a new assurance which He gives him of the care of His providence; but as this poor abandoned one had re-entered a little into himself by the care that he desired to take for the future, God draws him out still further, and by a simple comparison *of the stars,* He shows him the effects of His power, again assuring him that His promises are infallible, and that He is almighty to fulfil them.

Genesis.

6. *Abram believed in the Lord; and his faith was imputed to him for righteousness.*

Faith is what God looks at most : thus the *faith* of this person, continuing his *abandon* and leaving himself in God's hands, is considered by Him more than all the actions of righteousness not sustained by so great a faith ; for this is a faith animated by an excess of love. Then faith and *abandon* suffice him for every thing ; and he has nothing more to do than to live in them.

7. *God said unto him again, I am the Lord that brought thee out of Ur of the Chaldees, to give thee this land to possess it.*

In order to so much the more exercise his faith, and to maintain him in the *abandon*, God gives him new assurances of His promises ; but this soul, not being yet permanently established in *abandon* and faith, vacillates, and through infidelity demands signs, without considering that they are as much opposed to the perfection of faith as to its state of destitution, and that stopping the creature at something created, they hinder it from having only the support of the goodness of the Creator.

8. *Abram said, Lord God, how shall I know that I am to possess it?*

12. *And when the sun was going down, a deep sleep suddenly fell upon Abram, and a horror of great darkness seized him.*

God gives him a sign, but in a manner sufficiently showing him that his distrust has displeased Him : for nothing is so much opposed to faith and *abandon* as signs. The Divine moment must decide in everything, and the soul wait for this moment without seeing anything, without troubling itself to foresee anything for the future, not even when the time of the promises appears past. And the only way to avoid being deceived is to halt at nothing but at this moment of God's will, who is always infallible in His execution.

13. *Know of a surety that thy seed shall dwell in a strange land, and shall be reduced to slavery, and afflicted with diverse evils for four hundred years.*

As renouncement, faith, and *abandon* lead God to give great rewards, that it seems He has not wherewith to recompense these heroic virtues, otherwise than in giving Himself: so the least distrust, or desire for a sign, which is so much opposed to them, draws down His indignation, and obliges Him to threaten and punish even him whom before He had desired to recompense with Himself. Oh how mysterious this is, and how necessary for our instruction! for it is certain that often the faults that we commit against faith and *abandon*, for which we are immediately reprehended, strengthen faith more by the use that God makes of them than a pursued fidelity which has never experienced any weaknesses.

God then in a manner threatens Abram regarding his posterity, as the promises He had made were for the same posterity. The *horror and great darkness* point out the bad effects of signs and assurances that we seek for through infidelity, and which, casting the soul into fear and hesitation, form an obstacle to the graces of God, and to His Divine light.

14. *They shall come out of this land afterwards enriched with great goods.*

17. *When the sun went down, there was a great darkness.*

18. *And that day God made a covenant with Abram.*

Nevertheless God continues to fulfil His promises after seeing them dearly paid for, and the soul having re-entered the *darkness* of faith, as it is said that *after the sun went down it was dark*, God renews His *covenant* with it, and continues on its behalf the cares of a particular providence.

CHAPTER XVI.

1. *Sarai, Abram's wife, had yet borne no children.*

3. *And she took her maid Hagar, an Egyptian, and gave her to wife unto her husband.*

The inferior part, represented by the *wife*, tiring of so long a *barrenness*, and of so obscure and bare a road, seeks amongst strangers what she does not find with herself; and provided that she has a little support, she does not trouble herself where it comes from.

4. *Hagar, seeing that she had conceived, despised her mistress.*

5. *Then Sarai said to Abram, Thou wrongest me.*

6. *Abram answered her: Thy maid is in thy hand, do with her as thou wilt.*

She is not long in experiencing its penalty : for this support, which she has desired to take, is a *servant,* to whom she has given an advantage over herself, and who makes use of it to despise and wrong her. Then she sees her mistake, and complains to the superior part, whom she had made a participant in her fault, the latter re-establishes her in her place, and restores to her her authority, which she had allowed to be usurped.

11. *The Angel of the Lord said unto Hagar: Behold thou hast conceived, and wilt bear a son, and thou shalt call his name Ishmael, for the Lord hath heard thy affliction.*

Hagar represents the ways of multiplicity and activity, which we prefer to faith, because of the latter's apparent sterility. Although she is only a servant, she is yet to become mother of a great people in *Ishmael,* but of a people all full of trouble, wars, and divisions, and who obtain nothing but at the point of the sword : God recompenses thus *her affliction.*

13. *Hagar called upon the name of the Lord that spake to her, saying, Thou God seest me; for surely, she said, I have looked upon him from behind who sees me.*

God bestows some favours on these multiplied souls, but He only suffers them to *see* Him *from behind,* that is to say, in His gifts and images : and they can never arrive at union with Him by this way.

CHAPTER XVII.

1. *The Lord appeared unto Abram, and said unto him, I am the Almighty God, walk in my presence and be thou perfect.*

2. *I will make a covenant with thee, and will multiply thy seed even to infinity.*

God shows the soul abandoned to Him that He is *almighty,*

and that it ought to be content to *walk before Him*, in order to please Him in all things, seeing that this is the way to become *perfect.* He protests to it at the same time, that He will *unite Himself* to it, and will render it *fruitful;* which is, in the first place, to honour it with His Divine union ; then to enrich it with the productions of its own fruitfulness.

3. *And Abram fell on his face on the ground.*

This soul being instructed to no longer desire signs, thinks only of being annihilated, knowing that the most fit disposition for serving God's designs is annihilation, and that the true preparation for the supernatural is nothingness.

4. *And God said to him, It is* I WHO AM. *I will make a covenant with thee, and thou shalt be the father of many nations.*

After the mystic annihilation, God communicates Himself quite in another manner from formerly: for He gives to a heart perfectly submitted to Him, the greatest and most complete *knowledge* that can be had here below of His Divine Majesty ; saying that HE Is, and that nothing is without Him nor out of Him. He also renews *the union* and His promises.

5. *Neither shall thy name any more be called Abram, but thy name shall be Abraham: for a father of many nations have I made thee.*

6. *Kings shall come out of thee.*

It is then that there is *given the new name,* to wit, after the annihilation: a name that no one knoweth but he that receiveth it : a name given by the Lord from His own mouth, and consequently with everything necessary to complete its meaning. The promises are reiterated for a *numerous generation,* even exalting the merit and quality of the persons included in them, for it is added : *Kings shall come out of thee:* and it is said elsewhere that "he is the father of us all."

7. *And I will establish my covenant between thee and me, and thy seed after thee in their generations, for an everlasting covenant, to be a God unto thee, and to thy seed after thee.*

He assures this abandoned soul, after it has reached this

point, and has received the new name, that *He* will henceforth
be *its* God, and the God of all the abandoned souls that will
issue from it. It is then that there is established the true
stability: and there are no more changes for this soul. God
says that *He is their God*, and that His covenant with them will
be permanent, durable, and everlasting. He is their God,
for He commands them as a sovereign, and nothing resists Him
in them any longer, their will being lost in His own : and they
do His will on the earth as the blessed in heaven.

> 10. *Every man child among you shall be circumcised.*
> 12. *The child of eight days shall be circumcised among you : the
> slaves born in thy house, as well as those thou hast bought,
> or which are of a foreign nation.*

God gives a commandment as the sign of the covenant. He
expresses to us by it that in order to enter the way of *abandon*
we must labour by *circumcision*, or the cutting off of all that gave
us life in Adam. The beginning of the way of the spirit is
this continual mortification and renouncement of everything
that maintains the carnal and animal life ; by this we know
God's people. There is no longer any difference between *bond
and free*, for all conditions are equal for those who abandon
themselves to God.

By *the child born in the house*, is represented him whose life
has been innocent: there seems no retrenchment necessary for
him : nevertheless there is, and all are obliged at the beginning
to renounce everything of the life of Adam in order to give
place to the life of Jesus Christ. *The slave* signifies those who,
having groaned under the tyranny of sin, must, whenever they
give themselves to God, suffer circumcision. I confess that this
circumcision is more passive on their part than active : which
happens thus, because that, when they are fully abandoned,
God Himself operates with sword in hand, cutting off their
uncircumcision, without being arrested either by the grief, fears,
or tears of those who must suffer these wounds. The more
inveterately old sensuality becomes, like the foreskin, the more
it resists the knife, and circumcision is so much the more
severe. Those then who pretend to be abandoned, and who
nevertheless have not suffered the knife nor the cutting off of
their own life ; or who, having only the name thereof, wish to
preserve everything, and to lose nothing, are as much excluded

from the number of the true abandoned ones as from that of the truly circumcised.

> 15. *God said again unto Abraham : Thou shalt no longer call thy wife Sarai, but Sarah.*
>
> 16. *I will bless her, and give thee a son by her.*

God having renewed the centre of the soul and the superior part by the resurrection of the spirit after its mystic death, drawn as it has been from the region of the shadow of death, and established in the new life, typified by the new name : He now also renews the inferior part, *changing its name*, and making it participate in the renewal of the superior. Therefore some time after changing Abram's name *He changes Sarai's*, and makes to her the same promises as to her husband; He adds that she will bear him a son.

> 17. *Then Abraham fell on his face to the earth, and laughed, saying in his heart, Shall a man that is an hundred years old have a son ; and shall Sarah, that is ninety years old, bear ?*
>
> 19. *But God said to him, Sarah thy wife shall bear a son, and thou shalt call his name Isaac, and I will make with him and with his seed after him an everlasting covenant.*

The superior part, which had believed the promises made for itself, hesitates when there is promised that of its reunion with the inferior there is *to be born a son*, for whom all the promises have been made, knowing the feebleness of this inferior part, and regarding it as out of God, it *doubts* it, and at the same time the Divine power : pleading reasons derived from the long experience of their weakness, impotency, and sterility. These two parts live contented in their poverty, and desiring nothing more, hope for nothing more. This is the state of repose in God, preceding the Apostolic life. This *Isaac* that is to be conceived, is Jesus Christ formed in the souls : but He is only born when there is no longer anything in them that can create a just hope of conceiving Him. This infant is only conceived in the complete despair of all natural succour, and in a perfect disinterestedness for all supernatural gifts : so that, as says St. Paul, "the excellency of the power may not be attributed to man, but to God."

18. *And Abraham said unto God, Oh that Ishmael might live before Thee.*

20. *God said unto him, I have heard thee also regarding Ishmael : I will bless him and will multiply him exceedingly ; twelve princes shall come out of him, and I will make him the chief of a great people.*

Abraham by these words represents most perfectly the souls of faith that are in total nakedness. When they reflect upon their state, so poor and so destitute, Oh that it *might please God*, say they, for us to employ ourselves in holy activities, instead of remaining thus useless, and *that this Ishmael*, representing the multiplied practices, *might live* from *God* Himself. But God, seeing this error, affirms that He *has blessed* this way in everything He could, as much as it is capable of, and that it will possess great advantages : yet it is not to be that of His people, because it is the way of a people, not freed from the flesh, and His people are to be in Jesus Christ. For this reason He allows those who are to beget this people, so dear to Him, to attain even a hopeless age, so that they who will be born of them, as says St. John, "may be born, not of blood, nor of the will of the flesh, nor of the will of man, but of God."

As there is not a word in Scripture that may not serve for our instruction, it must be observed, that all the promises made for *Ishmael* are confined and limited to a certain *number :* but those made for *Isaac*, who is the figure of faith and *abandon* to God, are without limit: for he includes in his posterity nothing less than God Himself. Nothing less than God can be the recompense of a soul of faith : thus He Himself says to Abraham, " I am thy exceeding great reward."

CHAPTER XVIII.

1. *The Lord appeared to Abraham as he sat at the door of his tent, in the Valley of Mamre, in the heat of the day.*

This passage marks the assiduity of a soul to attract God and to preserve his possession, when it has found Him in the repose of contemplation. *Abraham sat in the Valley of Mamre :*

to sit, this is to be in repose ; we must be in repose that God may manifest Himself—be in repose *in the valley* of humiliation and annihilation.

> 2. *And lifting up his eyes he beheld three men near him.*
>
> 3. *And He said, Lord, if I have found grace in Thy sight, pass not by the tent of thy servant.*

This soul is not at all desirous of allowing its Beloved to depart, who has honoured it with His visit: on the contrary it longs to retain Him for ever. In this love that it has for its God, it believes everything to be God, and would treat every one as God Himself. It is then that He communicates Himself to it in such a manner, that it finds Him in everything. Thus Abraham treated those strangers who presented themselves before him, as God Himself: he is so filled with God, that he cannot say anything else. He speaks to three as to one : *Lord*, he says, *if I have found favour in Thy sight, pass not by the tent of Thy servant.* It is the same with this soul ; it finds God in everything, and everything is God for it.

> 6. *And Abraham hastened into the tent unto Sarah, and said, Make ready quickly three measures of fine meal, knead it, and make cakes upon the hearth.*
>
> 7. *And Abraham ran unto the herd, and fetched a calf tender and good, and gave it unto a young man, and he hastened to dress it.*
>
> 8. *And he took butter and milk with the calf that he had dressed, and set it before them.*

Those who are worthily touched by the love of God in the passive way of contemplation, find nothing difficult when His glory is in question ; nothing costs them an effort to give Him proofs of their love : thus they do everything with *speed* and activity, without, however, interrupting their repose; their liberality equals their love. Such was that of Magdalen at the house of Simon the leper.

> 9. *And when they had eaten they said unto him, Where is Sarah thy wife ?*
>
> 10. *In a year she shall bear a son. And when Sarah heard this, she laughed behind the tent door.*

12. *Saying to herself, After I am old, and my lord is old also, shall I yet have this pleasure.*

Their liberality is rewarded by the assurance of the near fulfilment of the promises: but they who are not made firm in God *hesitate*, returning from time to time to their doubts and distrusts, caused by reflections on their incapacity and weaknesses. As for those who are thoroughly established in God, they cannot hesitate or doubt any more. But, oh how rare these are upon the earth ! Where shall we find them?

What Sarah says: *After I am waxed old shall I have pleasure?*—meaning that she did not think to make use of marriage any more, shews that she regarded it still in a human manner and not in God.

13. *But the Lord said unto Abraham, Wherefore did Sarah laugh, saying, How could I have a child, being so old?*

14. *Is there anything too hard for the Lord?*

Abraham firmly fixed in the state of *abandon* and faith is the father of all those who have entered therein after him. He doubts no more : therefore he has no part in Sarah's fault: he believes it incumbent upon him to hope even against hope. This is the just praise that St. Paul bestows upon him. The Lord complains to him of the hesitation of his wife, bringing to his recollection that *nothing is impossible for God.* It is thus that He delights to exercise faith and *abandon*, granting things only when they are most despaired of. But the creatures not yet wholly drawn out of themselves *doubt* like Sarah, on account of looking at things from the side of reason ; in place of which the souls of pure faith regard them only from the side of God, to whom nothing is difficult.

15. *Sarah denied it, and said, I laughed not, for she was afraid. It is not so, said the Lord, for thou didst laugh.*

This creature still existing in herself, being reprehended for her doubt, desires to *justify herself;* and endeavouring to do so, inconsiderately falls *into lying. Sarah* commits two faults : the one, of lying ; and the other, that in order to excuse herself, she accuses God : for if it *be not true* that she laughed, she casts the lie back upon the Lord Himself who chides her for it. It is thus also with persons who are continually excusing themselves. They accumulate fault upon fault in their replies and hesitations, and then they cast back the fault upon God Himself, accusing Him of cruelty, or complaining that He abandons them and does nothing for them. But the soul of faith remains firm and constant in all His providences : and by this fidelity it draws the regards of God upon it with His greatest graces : thus St. Paul says, that "it was by faith that Abraham was blessed."

17. *And the Lord said, Shall I hide from Abraham that thing which I do :*
18. *Seeing that Abraham shall surely become a great and mighty nation, and all the nations of the earth be blessed in him.*

God could not *conceal anything* from His servant now established in naked faith and reposing in Him. He cannot but discover to him His secrets: and as he has the spirit of God, so also does he know what passes within the heart of God, and even the most hidden things of conscience, discerning immediately their states by a secret odour and a divine taste.

20. *The cry of Sodom and Gomorrah is great, and their sins have become very grievous.*
21. *I will go down now, and see whether their works are according to this cry which has come up to me. I will know whether it is so or not.*

Let us admire the manner in which God punishes sinners. He desires to *examine* everything Himself: for He seeks only to show mercy: He warns His friends of it, that they may prevail with Him if it is possible. But to bestow favours on His creatures, He anticipates them ; and to reward, He does not examine things so minutely: for His mercy surpasses His judgment.

23. *And Abraham drew near and said, Wilt Thou destroy the just with the wicked?*
24. *If there be fifty just persons in that city, shall they perish with the others ? And wilt Thou not rather spare the place on account of these fifty just persons should they be be found there ?*

Two of these angels go to Sodom, and the third, representing God, remains with Abraham, who always speaks to Him as to the Lord. We ought here to admire the ardent and efficacious manner in which the friends of God supplicate Him on behalf of His enemies. They lay themselves before Him as their advocates. They take God by the strongest and most touching points, making it appear to Him that there are some *just* persons, so that on their account He may pardon the criminals. But what are so few just among so many guilty? Nevertheless if they had been found, they would have saved the city. The servants of God press Him still by His justice itself, pointing out to Him, that He has never caused an innocent one to perish for the guilty. 25. *That be far from Thee, said Abraham, to do after this manner, to slay the righteous with the wicked; and that the righteous should be as the wicked, that be far from Thee.*

> 27. *Since I have taken it upon me, I will speak again unto the Lord, although I am but dust and ashes.*

The humility of him who supplicates in a profound *annihilation*, looking for nothing from other source than from the goodness of God, is of great weight before Him to obtain what is sought. Thus God promises him (verse 32) *that should only ten just persons be found in this city, it should not perish;* whilst Abraham, admiring the infinite clemency of God, dares not push his supplication further, doubting not but that Lot and his family are pardoned.

> 33. *And the Lord departed when He had left off speaking to Abraham, and Abraham returned to his own place.*

Two things are to be remarked here: the one, that as God cannot refuse anything to His best friends, and as, moreover, there are sinners in a final impenitence on account of their obstinacy, He does not permit His favourites to ask Him anything other than what He can and will grant them. It was for this reason that Abraham's prayer finished as above: and that God refusing him nothing, did not relinquish exercising His justice on this impious city. The other thing to be observed is, that persons who have attained this permanent state in God can only pray what He wills, and according as He Himself moves them, having no longer any other interests than His. This is visible in Abraham, who, forgetting all self-interest, and everything regarding flesh and blood, to abandon all to God, does not even enquire what will become of Lot his nephew in the vengeance that God will take on the city of his habitation. So much is he assured of God's goodness and justice. His own interests are nothing more to him than those of others, and everything has become for him one in God.

Abraham returns after this prayer *unto his place*, which is the repose in God, in which he was before seeing the three angel travellers.

CHAPTER XIX.

1. *There came two angels to Sodom at even, and Lot sat in the gate of the city, and when he saw them, he rose up to meet them, and bowing himself to the ground, he worshipped them.*

In the midst of so corrupt a city as *Sodom*, there is found one man who dwells in the repose of contemplation, and whom God delivers from the ruin destined for the wicked. *Lot* in his repose (for he is *seated*) marks the contemplative soul: and as being Abraham's kinsman, he is of the race of souls abandoned to God, so also he does what Abraham did on the preceding day, although in a much lower degree: for he still *sat at the gate of the city*, marking only an incipient contemplation, and yet little distant from the tumult of action: but Abraham seated at the door of his tent designates the repose in God free from all commerce with the creatures.

12. *The angels said unto Lot, Hast thou here any of thy relations, son-in-law, or sons, or daughters? Bring out of this city all that belong to thee.*

A contemplative soul, especially at the beginning, has yet a great many things binding it in commerce with the creatures, of which it has difficulty in ridding itself. This is why the angels are obliged to press Lot. But words are not efficacious enough; for the steps of these persons, although full of apparent fire and ardour, are yet slow and tardy as to the performance when there are many difficulties to surmount. It is necessary that God or His angels *take them by the hand* in order to protect them from the fall and ruin which would overwhelm them, if they did not come out from it speedily.

16. *And seeing that he still lingered, they took him by the hand, for the Lord was merciful to him, and they took also his wife and two daughters.*

17. *And they brought him out of the city, and said to him, Escape for thy life, look not behind thee, neither stay thou in all the plain, but escape to the mountain lest thou perish with the others.*

If God did not act thus, these persons are so little courageous, and still so feeble and attached, that they would never succeed. God, wishing to draw them from everything created, and to *conduct* them by His providence, bids them *look not behind them, nor stop at all.* These are the faults of persons in this state: either they look behind them, by reflection, or they stop at something less than God, through some reserve. The angels counsel them to leave off all commerce with the creature, *to get up upon the mountain*, which is the highest degree of contemplation.

18. *Lot answered them,*

19. *I cannot escape to the mountain, lest some evil befall me, and I die.*

20. *But here there is a city near to flee to. It is a little one, and it will save my life.*

Those persons who hesitate, *are fearful of their loss*, excuse themselves at first, and desire by measures of prudence to place themselves in safety. They propose a *city*, which they choose in order to be assured of a manner of life in which they can preserve and conduct themselves, not yet being able fully to trust themselves to God, and to abandon themselves wholly to His providence. They make even a specious pretext of the *littleness of the city*, as if to say : I prefer a lower and more sure way than these great states where there is more danger. They wish also to make God enter into this design by asking Him : *Is it not a little one*—this city that we ask for our security? Is it not the way of humility, which will give *life* to my soul?

Chapter XIX.

21. *The Angel answered him, I have heard thee concerning this thing. I will not overthrow this city for which thou hast spoken to me.*

God *hears* the prayers of these wavering souls, on account of their feebleness : and *grants them* what they ask, even miraculously.   This enraptures them, thinking that this request was agreeable to God, and advantageous for themselves : since He performs miracles on their behalf : but it is quite the contrary, it being only granted them on account of their weakness.

26. *Lot's wife looked behind her, and was changed into a pillar of salt.*

The soul that is not far advanced enters on reflection, and *looks behind it*, against God's commandment.   Nothing is so necessary in this way as to go on without reflecting : and God, in order to make an example, *changes this* feeble *woman* into a *pillar of salt;* showing thereby that *the salt*, that is to say, our own wisdom, prudence, and foresight is useless in a way where abandon and faith must alone conduct : and that all the measures that we are desirous of taking by ourselves, serve only to create a stoppage in the interior road, far from contributing some means of advancement therein.

29. *And it came to pass, that when God destroyed the cities of the plain, He remembered Abraham, and delivered Lot from the overthrow of the cities in which he dwelt.*
30. *Lot then withdrew into a mountain with his two daughters.*

God, for the sake of the perfect contemplative soul, delivers him who was only beginning, from the overturning of the city he had chosen for habitation.   Lot, by his prayers, or rather on account of Abraham, is inspired to *go up into the mountain*, where he dwells in *a cave with his two daughters :* this is the representation of the solitude of the contemplative.

33. *They gave wine unto their father, and made him drink that night.*

He believes himself covered from everything, having with him his *two daughters*, to wit, silence and retreat ; but he sees not that because he trusts too much in himself, they will be the

293

cause of his loss : God permitting it thus to shew him that it is in vain he thinks of taking care of himself if God Himself does not protect him, and to lead him by this to total *abandon,* into which he wishes to make him enter.

CHAPTER XX.

1. *And Abraham went to Gerar and dwelt there some time.*
2. *And he said of Sarah his wife, She is my sister. Abimelech King of Gerar sent for Sarah, and brought her to him.*
3. *But God appeared to Abimelech in a dream by night, and said to him : Thou shalt surely die if thou touchest the woman thou hast taken, for she has an husband.*
4. *Now Abimelech had not touched her. And he said, Lord, wilt Thou slay an innocent nation dwelling in ignorance.*

Abraham told no lie, saying that *Sarah was his sister,* since as he explains further on, she was truly his sister, being the daughter of his father although not the daughter of his mother : not, however, the immediate daughter of Terah the father of Abraham, but of Haran his brother. Thus Sarah was the granddaughter of Terah, and Abraham's niece : and Abraham could say that she was his sister, seeing that she was the granddaughter of his father, and that in Scripture the words son and daughter are often used for grandson and grand-daughter. The fault that he would seem to have committed would be to so often expose the life and honour of his wife. But besides the fact that a man of so great a faith does nothing but by the particular order of God, who moves him to act thus, there is more than that—that God permitted those things as they happened, in order to show to every one both the great faith of Abraham and the altogether particular protection of God over those who trust themselves to Him. It will be said that if Abraham's faith was great, and if the conduct of God was particular over him, He ought to have made him aware that Abimelech would not touch his wife, should he declare her as such. To that it is easy to reply, that besides that this is the manner in which God usually acts toward the souls whom He conducts by faith, to wit, making them go and come as He wills without, however, giving them any certitude of what is to happen, and that it is to exercise so much the more their faith and *abandon* that He thus conceals His designs from them : besides this, God desired to signalise His protection of those who unreservedly abandon themselves to Him, and to declare Himself on their behalf, in a striking manner, to serve for ever as an example to the souls of faith and to encourage their confidence.

5. *I have done this with a simple heart and pure hands.*

6. *God said unto him, I know that thou hast acted in this with a simple heart : therefore have I withheld thee from sinning against me, and have not suffered thee to touch her.*

It is certain that many people are persuaded of not being guilty on account of their ignorance, and nevertheless they are truly so. For to prevent sin two things are necessary — ignorance, and simplicity of heart : the latter is the most necessary. Therefore *God said* to Abimelech that *He had not permitted him to sin against Him, because of the simplicity of his heart.* God would sooner perform miracles incessantly than permit a person, who would go to Him in simplicity, to sin against him in ignorance, not only in sins of the spirit, but even material ones. according as it is added : *I have not suffered thee to touch her.* But it usually happens that those ,who sin through ignorance have the heart corrupted by other sins which they knowingly commit : therefore having no simplicity of heart, but on the contrary having the heart corrupted in everything, they sin even in things that they do not know to be sin, by reason of the depravity of their heart. From which it can be inferred, how much uprightness and simplicity of heart are advantageous for us. This is what God asks principally from us. It is simplicity which renders the heart pure and upright : and such a one as appears to commit faults does not do so, because of the simplicity of his heart : whilst those, who appear outwardly just, sin on account of the artifice and duplicity with which they act, and which is the source of hypocrisy.

9. *And Abimelech called Abraham, and said to him, Wherefore hast thou treated us thus ? What evil have we done*

> *thee that thou has brought on me and on my kingdom a great sin?*
>
> 11. *Abraham replied, I said to myself, surely they fear not God in this place, and they will slay me for my wife's sake.*
>
> 12. *And yet indeed she is my sister, being the daughter of my father, although not the daughter of my mother.*

The reproach that Abimelech makes to Abraham shows the innocence and simplicity of heart of this king, and the fear he had of displeasing God, which obliged the Lord to perform a double miracle in order to save the honour of Sarah and preserve this prince from crime. I have cited these passages designedly to make apparent the fidelity of God towards His little creatures when they are willing fully to trust themselves to Him, and abandon themselves to His care, always preserving a sincere desire of pleasing Him, and a real aversion to sin.

> 16. *And Abimelech said unto Sarah, I have given to thy brother a thousand pieces of silver that thou mayest always have a veil for thine eyes, before all with whom thou art, and wherever thou goest: and remember that thou hast been taken.*

Beauty, however chaste, may be violated if it have not a holy modesty which leads it to conceal itself. So holy a woman as Sarah had need of advice on this point for having affected to appear a maid, and not a wife: and a prince gives it to her wisely, although in an age in which God had not yet caused His law to be written, which ought to be graven only on the heart. How much more are similar cautions necessary for Christian women who suffer themselves to be seduced by the vanity of the age? And how much ought the guides of souls to be firm and inflexible in reprehending the immodesties and nudities which scandalise the Church so greatly? It is not sufficient to have the heart pure: exterior modesty is necessary to prevent the sins which others would commit on account of beauty too much exposed, although its possesser may have a heart very far removed from crime. *The veil,* which Abimelech gave to Sarah, is of the highest instruction for Christian women, who ought always to go veiled, particularly to churches. This is the counsel of St. Paul. We cannot have too much reservation on this point: for the exterior is often a sign of the corruption or purity of the heart.

Chapter XXI.

This *veil* has also a mystical sense altogether divine. It is that God caused a veil to be given to Sarah who was of her time the most favoured woman of God: to teach two things to interior persons; first, that they ought to preserve the gifts of God under the veil of silence and retreat; and secondly, that God makes use of naked faith as a veil to cover the gifts and favours He imparts to souls, and to keep them secure when He believes that His graces may expose them to be taken in the snare of the DEMON through vanity. Therefore Abimelech in giving Sarah wherewith to buy herself a veil said to her, *remember that thou hast been taken.* From that time there was no more danger for Sarah; as there is no more for a soul when naked faith has been communicated to it. That is its sure guard; for concealing from it its graces and virtues, it keeps it free from danger of taking some vain satisfaction in them, and consequently thus giving entrance to its ruin.

CHAPTER XXI.

1. *The Lord visited Sarah, as he had promised, and fulfilled his word.*
2. *For she conceived, and bare a son in her old age at the set time that God had spoken.*

Behold the *fulfilment* of God's promises, *in the time* that He hath appointed; and not always according to our views. The true interior life is begotten by faith, signified by Abraham; and it is brought forth by *abandon*, designated by Sarah. Abraham is then the father of all the interior souls; for " he is the father of all those who believe," according to St. Paul; and the interior and mystical life has its origin in faith.

3. *Abraham called the son that Sarah bare to him, Isaac.*
4. *And he circumcised him on the eighth day as God had commanded him.*
7. *Sarah nourished him with her milk.*

This interior infant is no sooner born, than faith begins to purify it, by *retrenchment;* whilst trust and abandon sustain it by their *milk.*

Genesis.

8. *The child grew, and they weaned him, and Abraham made a great feast on the day that he was weaned.*

When this interior new born child has been for sometime sustained by the sweet milk of sensible trust, it is weaned from it as to the savoury flow which caused the delights of its spiritual infancy, in order to have it no more but in essence. It cannot but experience grief at this; but faith is rejoiced and *makes a solemn feast* of it, for this first stripping causes the child to *grow* and advance in age in the spiritual life.

9. *And when Sarah saw the son of Hagar the Egyptian playing with Isaac her son, she said to Abraham:*
10. *Cast out this bond-woman with her son, for the son of a bond-woman shall not be heir with Isaac my son.*

When *Abandon* sees this little interior one which has been newly weaned from the sweetnesses and the milk of the spiritual life, going to seek amusement with the active and multiplied life; then it says to faith: *Cast out* entirely all that remains of the particular method and of multiplicity; and let my son have no commerce with those who are attached to them without being willing to pass beyond; for, being slaves of their own inventions, *they never inherit* God Himself, who is the heritage reserved for the free man, who is *my son*, and whom I shall conduct straight to God by my total *abandon*, so that he may find in Him alone his everlasting portion.

11. *This appeared hard to Abraham, because of his son.*

Abraham would preserve in his house this multiplied son, for he is also *son* of faith; but he is the son of faith in a manner comprised, possessed, and mixed with something of propriety; and not in a manner spiritual, imperceptible, and lost in God.

12. *But God said unto him, Hearken unto Sarah in all that she saith to thee; for out of Isaac shall thy seed come.*
13. *And also the son of thy bond-woman will I make the chief of a great people.*

God gives faith to understand, that it must abandon this son, who dwells much in nature, and must blindly follow all that *abandon* will bid it do. He declares to it that this must be the rule of its house; because it is from the son of *abandon* and faith that *its posterity must proceed.*

For this reason when scripture speaks of *Ishmael,* it separates him from Abraham, saying that he will be the *father of a great nation;* but when it speaks of Isaac, it affirms that in him Abraham will be the father of an innumerable nation, shewing that it is by this only son of blind *abandon* that faith can establish its posterity.

> 14. *Abraham rose up in the morning, and took bread and a vessel of water, and put them on Hagar's shoulder, and sent her away with the child. And she departed and wandered in the wilderness of Beersheba.*

Faith is contented with giving provisions to the multiplied life, for it cannot do without them; and these provisions are *bread* and *water,*—some support and nourishment, and some flow of sensible grace, so that it may be able to walk; but so soon as the water begins to fail, being its support, that is to say, the sweetness of grace, it loses courage. Hagar and her son *wandered in the desert;* which is, that the multiplied have never a fixed and straight road, as those who walk by simplicity and *abandon.* They go wandering from place to place, from subject to subject, from way to way; and so soon as the water of sensible grace fails them, they fall into discouragement, cease to walk, and stop short.

> 15. *The water in the bottle being spent, she left her son lying under one of the trees that were there.*
>
> 16. *And going away from him the length of a bow shot, she sat down, saying, I will not see my child die, and lifting up her voice, she wept.*

She *leaves her son under a tree,* that is to say, all her hope in the things of the earth; and then going away from him, she weeps for the loss that she believes she has sustained of all her productions. Must *I see perish,* says she, what I have produced with so much pain? But as the affliction of these souls makes them return to God, they cry to Him, and they sit down; which means that being weary of their inquietudes and groanings, they remain a little in repose; then God fails not to send them new graces and sweetnesses, so as to sustain them, and to make them pursue their road; without which they would abandon all.

17. *God heard the voice of the lad.*

19. *And at the same time He opened the eyes of Hagar, and she saw a well of water, and she went, and filled her vessel, and gave the lad drink.*

20. *God dwelt with him; he grew and dwelt in the wilderness and became an archer.*

The Lord *hears the voice of the lad,* this is to remember the good which this multiplied soul has endeavoured to do, and to console it by the compassion He has for its weakness. He causes it to *find water;* for everything is done in these souls by activity: thus have they only earthly water, and *they must go and fetch it themselves* and carry their own provision. This is what those do who are laden and filled with practices and anxieties and a multitude of thoughts. God continues to accept their little cares and to be with them; but He prepares them for war, and their industry has a great part in all they do. They live on what they take by labour or in the combat: nothing can better mark the active life than all this.

33. *But Abraham planted a wood in Beersheba, and called there on the name of the Lord, the Everlasting God.*

34. *And he dwelt for many days a stranger in the land of the Philistines.*

Abraham, father of believers and the man of the greatest faith that ever was, called on the name of God in all places; because he was in continual prayer, he left everywhere the marks of his invocation, of his prayer and sacrifice. Scripture here calls the Lord the *everlasting God,* to give us to understand that being always God, He must always be worshipped, prayed to, and called upon as God; and that thus our worship and prayer are to become everlasting. Therefore Jesus Christ has said Himself, "that we must pray always, and faint not," and St. Paul desires us to pray without ceasing. It is the state of faith solely that can render prayer continual.

God exacts yet another thing from the souls of faith, which is, that they be as *strangers* upon the earth, so that stopping at nothing created in the world, whether corporeal or spiritual, they may go direct to God. And it is to be for us a figure of the disengagement in which faith places the soul, that *Abraham remains* thus a *stranger upon the earth,* having no fixed abode.

God asks not this external from all the souls of faith, although He may exact it from some whom He desires to render true children of Abraham. But as for the internal, He wishes it from all persons who are conducted by faith and *abandon;* without which their state would not be true, but imaginary. The other souls conducted by gifts, and not by blind faith, are established in themselves, and are firmly there in repose, and very contented; but the souls of faith have no repose, since they entirely quitted themselves, coming out, like other Abrahams, from their country, the place of their parentage, to go into another land, which is God; giving themselves entirely up to be lost in their Creator; going on unceasingly—without resting, until they have returned unto the abode of their origin, according to the promise made to them when faith took possession of their hearts. For, from the time that it seizes upon them, it suffers them to take no repose, neither in themselves, nor in anything created; and it gives them to understand that everything must be looked at out of themselves, and that if they are faithful in following faith, however hard it may appear to them, they will not fail to succeed.

CHAPTER XXII.

1. *After these things God tempted Abraham and said to him:*
2. *Take Isaac thine only son, who is so dear to thee; and go unto the land of Vision, and there offer him to me as a burnt offering upon one of the mountains that I shall shew thee.*

God tempts Abraham, to make the last trial of his faith, and to test him to the utmost in total nakedness, and in the stripping of all supports; not only of human props, of which He had already stripped him previously, making him come forth from his country, but also of supports taken in God even, in all His benefits and promises. He spares nothing; and to render the thing more severe and this faith more magnanimous, to prove and purify his love, and to rid him of all self-interest, and of all foreign attachment, although most legitimate, He says to him: *Take thy son;* this word is very sweet: not only thy son, but

thine only son : how very dear to him must he then have been !
He continues :—*thy son whom thou lovest so tenderly ;* to make
even his love serve for its liveliest grief. He names him by
his name, *Isaac;* placing before his eyes all the sweetness of
this amiable victim, so as to make him conceive so much the
more of the greatness of his loss and to render it more sensible
to him. Then He adds, *come and sacrifice him to me upon a distant mountain.* Is it not that the length of the road may try his
faith the more? Isaac, who has always represented the passive
life, or contemplation, is to perish : faith must sacrifice this life,
and give it the deathblow, so that there may remain nothing
more that can hinder the total loss into God.

But far from so severe a temptation diminishing the faith of
this Patriarch, it takes again even a new vigour ; and although
so surprising a commandment as is given him, is contrary to
that which God had given to every one not to shed human
blood, and must horrify him, according to reason, in the fear of
committing a parricide. Yet faith bears all that; and trusting
itself to God above reason and faith, it sets about executing
what has been commanded it. By this incomparable faith,
Abraham offered his Isaac although he had received the promises for him, and he was his only son; and he offered him
after God had said to him, that it would be from Isaac that his
descendants would go forth : But he thought to himself, that
God could well resuscitate him; therefore he was given him as
a mysterious figure. It is thus that St. Paul extols the greatness of this sacrifice.

It is by these wise excesses that God sometimes tries the
greatness of the faith of those perfectly abandoned to Him.
The active life loses courage for a little thing; by the failing
of the water of sensible grace it is afflicted and halts; but faith
cannot be shaken even by the loss of what is dearest to it : It
must immolate itself, whilst activity grieves over the loss of its
productions. This difference between these two ways is very
real, and it could not be better explained than in these parts of
scripture, where we can see by the difference of these two sorts
of courage the distinction between these two ways, as it may be
noticed in the course of the whole history of Abraham, Hagar,
Isaac, and Ishmael.

3. *Abraham then rose up while it was yet night, and prepared
his ass, and took with him two of his servants, and Isaac*

Chapter XXII.

his son; and having cut the wood necessary for the burnt offering, he went unto the place where God had commanded him.

Oh surprising promptitude of Abraham, or of faith, in obeying! He waits not until the day be come; he sets out *when it is yet night.* The night marks equally his diligence and the obscurity of his faith, denuded of all lights, and signs: Faith disposes of everything itself: it causes itself to be accompanied by *servants,* but they cannot aid it in this. It *prepares the necessary wood for the sacrifice,* so that there may remain no pretext for eluding obedience, although in a matter which reason might regard as suspicious in many points. Oh fidelity and generosity of faith! It is truly on good grounds that it is the source and origin of a great people and of an innumerable multitude of saints so much the more admirable before God as they are the more hidden from men.

4. *On the third day he lifted up his eyes, and saw the place afar off.*

Oh admirable perseverance of naked faith exempt from reflections and windings, which so long a road could not make to waver, no more than the presence of so amiable a son, of whom Abraham must be the innocent parricide. All natural and divine reasons—ought they not to hinder him from pursuing this road, and make him turn back,—the fear of being deceived, of being mistaken, of committing a crime against God and a cruelty against so dear a son? But how very far removed from these reasonings is naked faith! It does not even regard them, it has no eyes to look upon them. The command alone of God sufficeth it, and it is sufficient for it to believe what He has commanded without even examining whether it believes it or not: it has only ears to hear. Oh Faith, which removest mountains, thou makest to be done even more impossible things!

5. *He said unto his servants, Await me here with the ass: my son and I only go yonder to worship, and will return again to you.*

He does not take his *servants* upon the mountain which is to be the place of sacrifice; they would be too incapable for that,

303

and would be scandalised at it. Let us by no means discover the secrets of the interior to those who serve God yet as hirelings. The ways of the purest faith can be trusted to those who, as its friends, serve it already without interest; but the extreme *abandons* are only for children, who as *Isaacs* merit learning the sacrifices which have God for their author, and of which they are to be the victims. Perhaps also Abraham left his servants for fear that from a false pity, they might trouble or hinder the execution of this generous and in appearance rash design.

> 6. *And Abraham took the wood for the burnt offering, and put it upon Isaac his son; and he took the fire in his hand and a knife, and they went both together.*

Which ought we here to admire,—the inflexibility of faith, pitilessly *loading* this poor victim, or rather the generosity of this soul in accepting the cross that is to consummate its sacrifice, represented so naturally by the wood which it is made to carry? Faith, the cross, and the burnt-offering go in company, and walk in concert to conduct the soul to suffering.

The *fire* and the *knife* must be united in order to immolate it and reduce it to ashes. Oh admirable figure of the interior, sustained by the word of Jesus Christ! "I am come," said He, "to bring fire upon the earth, and what do I wish except that it burn:" and further, "I am not come to bring peace, but the sword." The knife must kill, and the fire burn; and it is naked faith that commits in the soul all these ravages.

> 7. *Isaac said unto his father, Behold the fire and the wood, but where is the victim for the burnt offering.*

This question of Isaac's shows the ignorance in which faith conducts the soul until it has arrived at the place of suffering. Abraham's reply expresses the *abandon* to providence, which accompanies faith: and the docility of Isaac in making no further enquiries, marks the soul's fidelity in suffering itself to be blindly conducted by faith and abandon. But it would be a little thing for this generous soul—this innocent victim to allow itself to be led thus in obscurity, if, when it sees its death near and its loss inevitable, it changed conduct.

> 8. *Abraham replied, My son, God will provide for Himself a victim for His burnt offering.*

Chapter XXII.

9. *And having come to the place which God had showed him, Abraham built an altar, arranged the wood, and bound his son Isaac, and laid him upon it.*

This dear victim must let itself be *attached* to the cross by the bonds of faith: it must lower the neck under the knife without hesitating or lamenting. All this takes place in deep silence and profound death, which permits not the least relief to nature, not even a single sigh or groan. Oh truly, although the natural death of Isaac did not then follow, his mystic death was certainly accomplished, all hope having been taken from him, and all desire for life extinguished in him. The extinction of his own life in order to live no longer but in God, was the just price of this great sacrifice which he had accepted with his whole heart. Likewise the death of the ram was the figure of the mystic or mysterious death represented in Isaac; since this was really a mystic and mysterious death, as much on the part of Isaac with regard to Jesus Christ, as on the part of the ram that died for Isaac.

10. *And he took the knife in his hand, and stretched forth his arm to slay his son.*

11. *The Angel of the Lord cried unto him out of heaven, Abraham, Abraham! and he answered, here am I.*

12. *The Angel said, Lay not thine hand upon the child, and do him no harm. Now I know that thou fearest God; since to obey me thou hast not spared thine only son.*

The sacrifice was also entire on the part of faith : for Abraham, *lifting his arm*, was sincerely willing to immolate this son so dear to him. The manner and time which God makes use of to prevent the execution of this strange design, are admirable in showing the conduct that He exercises over souls of this degree. In the first place He waits for the very extremity before succouring them, for there are no longer either signs or assurances for them, but only the Divine moment, which causes things to happen and to be known only the instant that they are to be performed, and no sooner. In the second place, He makes them walk by this very thing in an entire loss : and in order to take from them everything distinct, He makes known to them things only as they happen.

This is also to try the purity of their love, which fears not to

305

lose all to do the will of God, even to committing apparent crimes through an excess of *abandon* and trust in His wisdom and power. This promptitude of God in succouring the souls of *abandon* and faith in the extremity of their need, augments their *abandon* and faith: and this *abandon* and this faith cause Providence to redouble His care over these persons so wholly abandoned to Him: thus are they truly the souls of Providence.

> 13. *Abraham lifted up his eyes and perceived behind him a ram caught by the horns in a bush, and he took him, and offered him up as a burnt offering in his son's stead.*

God often appears to desire the sacrifice of everything, although in the execution He is contented with the least part, thus He accepts the *ram instead of Isaac.*

> 15. *The Angel of the Lord called unto Abraham out of heaven the second time, and said to him,*
>
> 16. *I swear by myself, saith the Lord, that since thou hast done this, and for love of me hast not spared thine only son,*
>
> 17. *I will bless thee, and will multiply thy seed as the stars of heaven, and as the sand that is on the sea shore: and thy posterity shall possess the gates of its enemies.*

God does not delay rewarding so liberal a sacrifice as this of his servant. And as this mystic death has been achieved by the real death and destruction of the victim—the ram, which was the figure of it, having been annihilated and reduced to ashes : so does God bestow upon this faithful soul new favours, and much greater than the first. It must be observed, that since immolation and sacrifice have been spoken of, all promises have ceased, and Scripture says nothing approaching to them : on the contrary these holy patriarchs walked in death : and by this very immolation all the promises that had been made to them appeared vain and useless, since they saw that everything was going to be destroyed for them : but naked faith has no more regard for blessings and past favours, nor for what has been promised to it: if it remembers them, this remembrance augments its death; for the soul cannot see them in itself, nor take anything of them for itself. But so soon as the sacrifice is finished, and the soul annihilated, God restores to it all its goods, and much more than it had before, but quite in another manner: for it has them no more in propriety, and it regards them no more as its own, but as belonging to God and being in Him.

When it is said to Abraham, that *his posterity will possess the gates of its enemies*, it is to signify that the soul which formerly had enemies extremely adverse and cruel to it, finds itself through its annihilation so strong over them, that it rules them, and holds them subject and as it were imprisoned: for to possess the gates of the place where the enemy is shut up is to hold him prisoner, and to become his master. So also these souls can no more fear the demon, since God, to whom they have unreservedly abandoned themselves by a generous love, has rendered him subject to them.

18. *All nations shall be blessed by him that shall come out of thee, for thou hast obeyed my voice.*

This expresses the inconceivable blessings God bestows on others on account of those persons so fully abandoned to Him. The greatest blessing is to make use of them for the formation of Jesus Christ in hearts: for it is *by Him* that *all the holy nations are blessed.* Therefore, as St. Paul remarks, "when God made His promises to Abraham and his son, He said not, to thy sons, as if speaking of many, but to thy son, as speaking of one alone who is Jesus Christ.

CHAPTER XXIII.

1. *Sarah lived one hundred and twenty-seven years,*
2. *And she died in the city of Arba. Abraham mourned for Sarah and wept for her.*

After faith and *abandon* have operated the mystic death, there must yet be lost this same *abandon*: it must die, not as to what there is real in it, which is even so much the more perfect, the more it is hid in God: but as to what it perceptibly had, and as to the facility of producing actions from it; for that being yet an obstacle to annihilation, it must be taken away. It is thus then that *abandon* dies, represented by *Sarah*, that is to say, that this soul, through having abandoned itself, loses all power of doing so any further: for it enters into God, where it dwells in total destitution, and where *abandon*, which had until now aided it to enter therein, leaves it. It costs it some *tears*, seeing that it can no more abandon itself: for it takes that as a more certain sign of its loss: but when it is established in destitution and loss into God, the pain ceases, and *abandon* being no longer perceived, is purer than it ever was before.

3. *Abraham said to the Children of Heth,*

4. *I am a stranger and a sojourner with you, give me as one of yourselves possession of a burying-place, that I may bury my dead.*

5. *The Children of Heth answered him,*

6. *Hear us, my lord, Thou art as a prince of God amongst us: choose of our sepulchres what pleases thee.*

There are Princes of God, and there are Princes of the world. Those of the world have authority only in their estates, and yet they are usually the slaves of those they rule over: since without them they can neither subsist nor defend themselves, nor undertake anything: but the Princes of God, who, as His children have entered into His freedom, are sovereign and mighty in the very place of their exile. They rule every one and are ruled by none. They are *as strangers with* men: but they are independent of the same men, and have a certain authority and gravity which surprise and oblige those who see them, and who do not comprehend this mystery, to look upon them with respect. The reason is that they bear the stamp of Divinity, as Princes bear the marks of their human authority. *Abraham*, whom the excess of his faith rendered *a stranger* and wanderer in the world, so that he might have no other country save heaven, who left his hereditary possessions in his fatherland, that God Himself might become his heritage,—Abraham, I say, is Sovereign Prince wherever he dwells. His independence makes itself known on all occasions. He enriches everybody, and receives nothing from any one, as he said to the King of Sodom, that "it should not be said that any one had enriched Abraham." Oh how rich he is who has God alone for his portion! It is the property of faith to impoverish in order to enrich, and to strip of everything so that God Himself may be our riches. David had experienced this happy state of denuded faith when He said : " The Lord is the portion of my inheritance;" adding afterwards : "the lines are fallen unto me in pleasant places : yea, I have a goodly heritage."

CHAPTER XXIV.

1. *Abraham was old, and already well advanced in years, and the Lord had blessed him in all things.*

2. *And he said to his eldest servant,*

3. *Swear unto me by the Lord, the God of heaven and earth, that thou wilt not take a wife unto my son of the daughters of the Canaanites, amongst whom I dwell,*

4. *But that thou wilt go into my country, and to my kindred, there to take a wife unto my son.*

This marks the perseverance of faith, and as since it has established the soul in God, it draws down upon it all kinds of blessings, for the soul essentially united to God is loaded in God Himself with all manner of good ; and as faith alone can conduct the soul into God Himself, it is by it that the soul is *blessed in all things.* But so ample a blessing is only accorded to it when it is already *very old,* I mean in its consummation.

The *country of the Canaanites* is the figure of the corrupted world. It is never there that faith makes an alliance : it loves to ally itself to the people that fear God, although they may be in multiplied ways : hoping that, as they have already quitted sin, it will the more easily be able to reduce them to its unity. It calls for this purpose all its old servants. The *eldest servant* of faith is prudence, which is the first faithful servant that serves it on its road, and which, nevertheless, would become afterwards most troublesome to it, if it did not know to change it, as will be shown further on. This *servant* is the eldest and the most necessary to faith at its beginning, for it leads it to abandon itself to God by a holy prudence, which causes us, seeing our affairs going wrong in our own hands, to put them into the hands of God by a total *abandon.* It is this prudence which, according to the sage, is " the knowledge of the holy :" this then must be the office of a true prudence. Faith, however, seeing that prudence, which has been so useful to it up to this point, is becoming extremely hurtful when, after the abandon to God, it desires to unite itself to human foresight, calls it in the person of *Eliezer*, and makes it *swear* that it will never make an alliance of the already advanced interior life with the world : which could not be without making the most detestable of all mixtures ; but that it will *go into the country* of the children of God, although still multiplied, which is the place whence faith itself takes its origin, so that it may there ally *its son*, the interior and already mystical life, born of *abandon* and faith.

5. *The servant replied, If the woman will not come into this country with me, must I bring back thy son into the land from which thou camest.*

Careful Prudence takes its precautions afar off, and would desire, in case there should be found no souls willing to enter into the interior ways (which is the alliance that faith desires to make), to *bring back* the already advanced interior man, figured in *Isaac*, into the multiplied ways sooner than leave him alone in the one and simple way : although God had drawn him from them in his father even before his birth. For faith is what takes hold of the soul in multiplicity to conduct it into unity ; and communicating to it the germ of its own life, places it beyond the power of ever returning to its ancient origin, at least without violating God's order over it, and going contrary to His will.

6. *Abraham said unto him, Beware that thou bring not my son into that country again.*

7. *The Lord, the God of heaven, who brought me out of the house of my father, and out of the land of my kindred, who spake unto me, and sware unto me, saying, Unto thy seed will I give this land: He shall send His Angel before thee, that thou mayest take a wife unto my son from thence.*

Faith, which never abandons this soul until it be in God, where, after seeing all lost, it re-finds everything in perfect unity, says firmly : *Beware*, Oh prudence, of ever conducting my son into the country of multipl.   ·, *out of which God has drawn us* in His infinite goodness. I _ave this confidence, that the *Lord of heaven* and earth, *who has taken me from my father's house,* from the way and commerce with the creatures in which I was born, *and who sware unto me to give me this land* of repose in God, and not only to me, but also to all those of my children who will follow the same way by which I have conducted my Isaac —the model of souls abandoned and sacrificed to the supreme will of God : The Lord, I say, *will send his angel before thee,* and will dispose all things, so that the spouse and faithful companion destined for my son, may enter into the same way with him, and may likewise possess the land of peace and repose in God, which they must leave to the posterity to be born from them. The angel here spoken of is Providence ; it is then that there begins the spiritual alliance.

8. *And if the woman will not be willing to follow thee, then thou shalt be clear from this my oath : only bring not my son thither again.*

9. *The servant bound himself by oath to perform what Abraham had commanded him.*

Faith   ̣s to Prudence, that *if this woman,* whom it is sent to choose, *will not come, it is freed from all oath,* provided that *it bring not back* its son, and that it leave him in repose and union, for that being chosen for the Divine repose, they must never, under any pretext whatever, return to multiplicity. This agrees with what is said elsewhere: " If ye keep my covenant, then ye shall be a peculiar treasure unto me above all people : ye shall be my priestly kingdom, and the holy nation that shall be consecrated to me." Upon which prudence swears to faith never to draw the abandoned soul from its way.

10. *And the servant took ten camels from the flock of his master, and took with him of all his goods, and he departed, and went into Mesopotamia, to the city of Nahor.*

He loads *ten camels*, representing the ten commandments of the law to be given to Moses, and which are observed interiorly by the mystics in a much more perfect manner than are the exterior, expressed simply by the letter. He loads them *with all his master's goods,* that is to say, with a great increase of graces which this way had drawn to it : so that love, faith, confidence, and all the virtues were so many riches that covered and sweetened the rigour of the law : they bring to her, moreover, all the goods of the house that is offered to her, so that concealing from her nothing of all the advantages of this way so simple, yet so rich, they may be able easily to attract her to it, and make her enter therein with pleasure. Mesopotamia is the country where people fear God though in multiplicity. Thence are drawn the docile persons, so as to introduce them into the country of peace and union.

11. *And he made his camels rest without the city by a well at even time, at the time when the women went out to draw water.*

12. *And he said, Lord God of Abraham my master, I pray Thee, help me this day, and show mercy to my master Abraham.*

The arrival of him who is sent to draw this woman (figure of the soul) from her multiplied state, is made in *the evening:* marking by that, that she was already in a repose half begun, or approaching repose, being at the end of the day of her activity; for God sends thus, when it is time, some person who points out the simple way. He seeks her *near the well,* that is to say, in the very practice of prayer, where she endeavours with all her strength, as do the young souls, to draw up the water of grace. *He makes the camels rest without the city:* to show that the graces coming of the passive faith, are not given in the tumult but in repose. And afterwards, addressing God, he makes his prayer to Him, in which this servant, albeit so wholly God's, speaks not of himself; he *entreats* Him only by *his master Abraham,* and on his behalf: for he knows that faith can obtain everything.

13. *Behold, I stand here by the well of water: and the daughters of the men of the city come out to draw water.*

14. *Let it come to pass then that the damsel to whom I shall say, Let down thy pitcher that I may drink : and who will answer me, Drink, and I will give thy camels drink also; let the same be she that Thou has destined for thy servant Isaac. Thereby shall I know that Thou hast showed mercy unto my lord.*

312

Chapter XXIV.

He asks of God that amongst so many persons following the same way, He may make known to him her whom He destines for the repose. But the condition in his prayer is wholly admirable and mysterious. He sees that all that can make the soul come forth from the country of multiplicity, to make it enter into the divine unity, is charity; that this charity is to be united to the abandoned soul, and that it is it that causes it to exist in a well purified love, although in the obscurity of faith. Therefore it is only charity which Eliezer seeks for Isaac, not an ordinary charity, but an abundant charity, fit to *water the flock* of Jesus Christ, included in Abraham. This is a mystery which would require a volume for its explication. And as the generosity of love performs more than is asked of it, this charity finds water to give to all according to their wants. This part of Scripture is enrapturing, seeing that everything relates so fitly to the interior conduct. It was necessary that the *wife* of Isaac be mother and nurse of the people of faith : therefore she is to be charity, that is to say, to give us in her person and conduct an excellent figure of it.

15. *Hardly had he finished these words, when, behold Rebecca appeared, daughter of Bethuel, the son of Milcha the wife of Nahor, Abraham's brother, bearing her pitcher upon her shoulder.*

16. *And the maid was very beautiful, neither had any man known her; and she went down to the well, and filled her pitcher and came up.*

Oh promptitude of God in hearing prayers made with faith when they are so just ! The young girl came then immediately that Eliezer had finished his prayer.

She was very beautiful: for nothing is so beautiful as charity, which renders itself agreeable to all. She was a *virgin;* for charity is always pure; and having her origin in God Himself, she preserves herself always chaste in the midst of the creatures, without sullying herself by their commerce. She *went down to the well, and filled her pitcher:* charity is always accompanied by humility, which in emptying itself grows full : and like a fountain, the more it empties itself of its waters, the more the source, which is God Himself, communicates to it new waters. This is what makes these two virtues, represented under this mystery, absolutely necessary for the soul destined to *abandon*

313

and unity in God, for the fidelity of charity consists in being always full for others, and retaining nothing for itself; and the perfection of humility is to empty itself unceasingly of the waters of grace, communicated to it, and to return them to God as pure as it receives them from Him.

Scripture says that Rebecca *returned again:* marking by that that although charity is beneficent to all, nothing, however, stops her: and that although she may go away quickly, she does not cease showing what she is, by doing good so soon as it is asked of her, and even sooner than that.

17. *The servant went before her, and said to her, Give me, I pray thee, a little of the water thou bearest, that I may drink.*

18. *And she answered, Drink, my lord, and letting down her pitcher upon her arm, she gave him to drink.*

19. *She added, I will draw water for thy camels also.*

20. *And she poured water from her pitcher into the trough, and ran to the well to draw another, and drew for all the camels.*

Who will not admire the grace and promptitude with which she does everything ? She *wishes* even *to give water to all the camels,* for it is charity that waters and vivifies the law, represented by the camels. She does not cease until she has filled them with her water, for the law without her would be void: she has no sooner *emptied* her pitcher than she goes to fill it from the source, from whence she draws all her goods. Charity does not content herself with words: she comes from them to deeds, truly *giving water to all the camels,* as she had offered.

21. *Still the servant looked upon her without saying anything, to see whether the Lord had made his journey prosperous or not.*

He *contemplated her,* says Scripture, so well: for he was of the house of faith, of which even the servants are contemplatives. He looked upon her in silence, showing the repose and silence of contemplation ; and he contemplated thus in silence, *to see whether the Lord had made his journey prosperous or not.* He does not interrogate this young girl: he does not make use of the multiplicity of discourse to be enlightened as to his doubt: he only employs repose, by which he is better instructed than he had been by all the cares. Likewise did he also hesitate before speaking to her.

> 22. *And after all the camels had drunk, he drew out golden ear-rings, weighing two shekels, and bracelets of ten shekels weight.*

He gives to her of his riches, to make known to her by deeds, much more than by words, the way and country to which he desires to attract her. But what are the presents he makes to her? *ear-rings;* to make her comprehend, that there is now no other thing necessary for her but to hear and be silent; and that that is the practice of the country to which he wishes to conduct her. He gives her also *bracelets* for her hands; so as to make her understand that faith, silence, and good works, must be inseparable from charity; from all this she is to learn to hear, to act, and to be silent. She accepts this pledge as a mark that she is disposed to enter on this way, if obedience permit it to her. The ear-rings are of *gold*, to mark the purity with which we must listen to God: they only *weigh each one shekel*: showing that we must listen only to God Himself and His holy will: but *the bracelets* weigh *several shekels of gold:* for virtues and good works must be multiplied. The attention must be fixed on God alone: but practices are extended towards all.

> 23. *And he said to her, Tell me, I pray thee, whose daughter thou art? Is there room in thy father's house for me to lodge?*
>
> 24. *She said to him, I am the daughter of Bethuel, the son of Milcha, the wife of Nahor.*
>
> 25. *There is with us straw and provender enough, and room to lodge in.*

Prudence, which never hastes, leads the servant to enquire of this young girl *who she is:* she tells him; and he asks her, *if there is room to lodge in her father's house?* Charity, which is never empty, assures that at the house of her father (who is the figure of God) there is wherewith to *provide for all*, and infinite space to lodge and well receive all who have recourse to her.

26. *And the man bowed down his head and worshipped the Lord.*

27. *And he said, Blessed be the Lord, the God of my master Abraham, who has not failed to show mercy on him according to His truth, and who has led me straightway into the house of my master's brother.*

Prudence *worships* God, admiring how faith is never destitute of truth, and how God makes everything succeed happily with it, for there is nothing which conducts so direct as this same faith. This servant is all astonished that for having blindly followed it, he has been *conducted by a straight road* to the most desired place, and that he has found much more than he had dared to hope. This is what leads him to render justice to the truth of the way of faith, and to proclaim how straight and sure it is. He does not know what most to admire, the providence of God in providing for everything at the proper moment, or the generosity of faith in undertaking everything in obscurity and without assurance. He sees too how God blesses faith with so many graces that he cannot forbear being struck with it and constrained to worship God in all His ways.

29. *Rebecca had a brother called Laban, and he ran out to the man, unto the well.*

31. *And he said to him, Come in, thou blessed of the Lord, why remainest thou without ? I have prepared the house, and room for thy camels.*

Laban seeing the pledges given to his sister, and which are the witnessings of the way of faith, comes out and seeks him who teaches her, to make him *enter into the house.* It happens as much thus to persons of good will when they obtain knowledge of these ways : they long to possess them and to introduce them to themselves : they receive them with pleasure, and protest that they have prepared with their best the *house* of their heart for their reception.

33. *They set meat before him, but the servant said, I will not eat until I have told mine errand.*

They hasten quickly to *give him meat to eat ;* but he, instructed in the ways, says : *I will not eat until I have told mine errand :* for such is the will of the Lord. Oh faithful servant, forgetting his own interests and pressing needs to think only of executing the desires of God.

34. *And he spake to them thus, I am Abraham's servant.*

35. *The Lord hath blessed my master very greatly, and hath made him rich and powerful.*

36. *And Sarah his wife bare unto him a son in her old age, to whom my master hath given all that he had.—Etc.*

When he expatiates upon *the riches of his master* and the favours that God has bestowed upon him, he extols the magnificence of this way, and how much God blesses it, making it appear elevated above all others. For, although prudence has very little experience of faith in its progress, nevertheless it is obliged to admire it in its successes. He declares its origin, and shows that there is nothing hidden for it, for faith having *given all* that it possesses to it, has convinced it of its truth. He adds that abandon is the mother and nurse of this same way.

He imparts to them all the secrets of faith, so as to constrain them by that to give themselves to it, by making the recital of all Abraham had said to him, and all that had passed near the fountain.

50. *Bethuel and Laban answered and said, It is God that speaketh here; we can only answer thee what pleaseth Him.*

51. *Rebecca is in thine hands; take her with thee that she may be the wife of thy master's son, as the Lord hath ordained it.*

The efficacy of grace is so great in the mouth of an interior person, that they *cannot* refuse him anything, nor *reply to him;* and *they are constrained to confess* that all comes *from God,* whom it is difficult to resist. These relations are then constrained by a gentle violence to give their consent, after which charity is truly united to the way of abandon. And at the same time there is made the all divine spiritual *marriage* of the Bridegroom and Bride, who are united to finish their course in the interior way, and to lose themselves happily in God.

53. *The servant brought forth vessels of silver and gold, and*

raiment, and presented them to Rebecca ; and he made presents also to her brethren and to her mother.

Then God displays all His riches to decorate and enrich His spouse.

But although He is almighty, He wishes, however, the consent of the spouse before making her wholly abandon her first way, denoted by her father's house ; and causing her to embrace this one, which introduces her by simplicity into the depths of the interior.

58. *And they called Rebecca, and said unto her, Wilt thou go with this man ? and she said, I will go.*

She agrees willingly, *replying* without artifice. This single word, *I will go*, suffices to express everything in a soul beginning to be instructed in the ways possessed by faith, and which are all simple.

60. *And they blessed Rebecca, and said unto her, Thou art our sister, be thou the mother of thousands of millions, and let thy seed possess the gate of those which hate them.*

Rebecca's relations having received considerable presents on account of her, teaches us how advantageous it is to be united to charity ; for we participate also in its felicity, and all those connected with persons so cherished of God, receive singular graces by it. They afterwards *bestow a thousand blessings* upon this dear sister, *wishing her fruitfulness*, and that *she may possess the gates of her enemies*, which is the very blessing God gave to Abraham, and has been explained above (chap. xxii. ver. 17).

62. *Isaac walked in the road leading to the well of the Living and Seeing.*

63. *He had gone out to meditate in the field at even, and lifting up his eyes, he saw the camels at a distance.*

Isaac went towards the well of the Living and Seeing, that is to say, near the spring that is in God, who alone lives and sees. He walked in God ; for the breadth of his soul was not straitened. He had come forth out of himself to better occupy himself with God alone. It was in this admirable intercourse that all-pure charity was brought to him, to be united to him by an indissoluble bond. He goes to meet her when he perceives her. Pure love is only granted to a soul when, having come out of itself, it occupies itself with nothing but God; and this happens only *towards the evening*, in the latter period of life, and after great labours.

64. *And when Rebecca perceived Isaac, she came off her camel.*

65. *And she forthwith took her veil and covered herself.*

She *comes off her camel* to go to him still more speedily; but she *covers herself with her veil*, which is fidelity; and thus equipped she goes to be united to him.

67. *Then Isaac brought her into the tent of Sarah his mother, and took her for his wife: and he loved her so much, that he moderated his grief, which the death of his mother had caused him.*

But what does Isaac? He does not amuse himself admiring the beauty of Rebecca, being already advanced in the way of faith, which has nothing sensual: but *he takes* her straightway *into the tent of his mother;* which is to make her enter into total *abandon*, which has been always represented by Sarah. And this *abandon* is the disposition immediate to union and to the enjoyment of the spouse. Therefore he makes her take that way. But having known the merit of charity, which renders the soul one in God alone, *he loves her so much that he forgets by that his grief caused by the death of Sarah*, which was the loss of abandon, which then became useless to him, being confirmed by charity in perfect destitution in God.

CHAPTER XXV.

1. *Abraham took another wife, named Keturah, who bare him six sons,*

5. *But he gave to Isaac all that he possessed.*

6. *He made presents to the sons of his other wives, and separated them during his life from his son Isaac, sending them into the country looking towards the east.*

Abraham had yet other children, but they had no part in the inheritance. Faith has many children to whom it gives some goods; but the *one Isaac,* son of naked faith and blind *abandon,* is the inheritor of all its riches. Those of the other ways have a share as servants, and have not a like habitation with him : Isaac is treated as an only son, and has nothing less than God Himself for heritage, since God was the possession of faith and *abandon,* of whom he is born. No soul ever arrives at the enjoyment of God, before being stripped of all support and all self-interest.

8. *And Abraham began to fail and died in a good old age.*

9. *And Isaac and Ishmael carried him to the Cave of Macpelah in the field of Ephron,*

10. *And buried him there, as he had done Sarah his wife.*

Abraham, the image of faith, having united his son to charity after conducting him by *abandon* and naked faith into God Himself, *begins to fail,* and faith itself *dies.* This patriarch having passed in substance into his son, and through him into all his descendants, all view of faith and all use of this light remain as dead and buried for the soul arrived in God Himself: because that all means, even the most necessary and most holy, finish when we have arrived at the last end. Then there is nothing for this soul to do but to enjoy pure charity in God Himself with an admirable purity and simplicity. And this is what precedes the Apostolic life, which is one and multiplied. For as God acts in everything without coming out of Himself or His unity, so also do these souls act outwardly without coming out of their unity in God. *Abandon* and faith are left at the same place, to wit, on arriving in God Himself.

Isaac remains with his spouse in this same place after the death of his father ; since there could not be other abode for such a soul than that, though it should traverse the whole earth ; for it might go throughout all the world without coming out of its place : thus it is added, that (v. 11) *after the death of Abraham God blessed his son Isaac, who dwelt near the well of the Living and Seeing.*

21. *Isaac prayed the Lord for his wife, for she was barren; and the Lord heard him, and Rebecca conceived.*

Charity reunited in God alone is in so perfect a repose, that she thinks no more of producing fruits abroad if she was not awaked from her gentle slumber by the occasions which providence gives rise to; for she possesses in herself all the blessings. *Isaac* her spouse *prays*, and *God immediately hears him*, giving him two children who become two very different peoples. Angels are lost in heaven: an apostle perishes in the company of Jesus Christ: and charity seems here to conceive and to bring forth a reprobate.

But as everything contributes to the glory of God and to the good of the chosen ones, according as a holy people is conceived in the bowels of charity, she conceives also a perverse people to try the former and make it suffer. To conceive and bring forth the race of the predestined, is to conceive and bring forth persecution and crosses. This nation, so holy, was persecuted before coming to the light, and suffered rude attacks before being born. There is no place exempt from the cross for the predestined, God makes them find it everywhere, it is born with them, it grows with their steps, and must be upon them until they expire.

22. *But the two children with which she was big struggled within her womb; which caused her to say, If this was to happen to me, why did I conceive? She went to inquire of the Lord.*

The soul not yet rendered firm in the experience of the ways of God *is afflicted* at seeing persecutions being born: and her grief obliges her to *consult the Lord*. This is the pious custom of the saints, to have recourse to God in their doubts and troubles; for all their trust is in Him. The example of all the patriarchs in this point shames Christians, who for the most part consult only the world or passion.

23. *God answered her, Two nations are in thy womb, and two peoples will come out of thy bowels, which shall be divided the one against the other; and the one people shall overcome the other; and the elder shall serve the younger.*

God consoles her, representing to her that it is necessary for it to be thus; and that after He has permitted the wicked to try the predestined, then they will be subjected to them; and the predestined who appear the *smallest* on account of their humiliations, will become *masters of their enemies*.

24. *When the time was come that she should be delivered, behold she was big with twins.*

There were found then *two children* in the same womb, the persecutor and persecuted ; and by exchange master and servant. He who persecutes is the slave of his passions, whilst the persecuted enjoys an admirable freedom and peace. The good and the wicked have truly issued from the same womb of Divine power by the creation, and yet the wicked do not cease opposing God and the good. Sin alone makes this division.

25. *He that came out first was red and all covered with hair, and was called Esau. The other came out after him, holding in his hand his brother's heel : therefore was he called Jacob.*

The persecutor *comes out first*, whose aspect is as fierce as his disposition is to become ; and as he is to be inhuman and cruel, he bears even upon his body the marks of a natural ferocity.

27. *When they grew, Esau became a cunning hunter, and loved to till the ground. But Jacob was a simple man dwelling in tents.*

Esau exercises his cruelty upon the animals which he takes *in the chase :* but Jacob, gentle and *simple*, tastes the repose of solitude, and imitating Jesus Christ beforehand, he exercises himself in retreat and prayer before applying himself to external employment. Grace leads to retreat and repose, until the Divine calling obliges us to put ourselves forward.

28. *Isaac loved Esau, for he ate of what he took in the chase; but Rebecca loved Jacob.*

Isaac loved Esau with some interest. It is so rare that one acts from pure grace, without any pursuit of self. The most holy are sometimes mistaken in the choice of their friendships: this choice is never perfect when interest, however so little, is mixed in it. But charity *loved Jacob*, because he was after God's heart ; and having no self-interest, her love was accompanied by justice and sustained by equity.

30. *And one day Esau said unto Jacob, Give me of this red pottage which thou hast made ready; for I am very faint.*

31. *Jacob answered him, Sell me then thy birthright.*
33. *And Esau sware unto him, and sold him his birthright.*

This is an admirable conduct of God, making His creatures, even the most rebellious, serve His designs. Everything happens as if it was not premeditated, and by the most natural providences. God permits Esau to dispossess himself of the *right* that he had over his younger brother, and *to sell it to him* for a little sensuality, which is, to eat a mess of *pottage*. All this, which appears so unreasonable and inconsiderate, serves God's design, who never violates our freedom, but who conducts all things gently to their ends.

CHAPTER XXVI.

1. *And there came a famine over that land, as there was one in the time of Abraham. And Isaac went to Gerar to Abimelech, King of the Philistines.*

2. *For the Lord had appeared unto him and said to him, Go not into Egypt, but dwell in the country which I shall show you.*

3. *Sojourn in this land, and I will be with thee, and will bless thee; for unto thee, and unto thy seed, I will give all these countries, and I will perform the oath which I sware unto Abraham thy father.*

4. *I will multiply thy children as the stars of the heaven, and all nations of the earth shall be blessed in him that shall come out of thee.*

At whatever degree of grace the soul may have arri d, it often experiences privations, which are kinds of *famine;* bu there is a time when they are no longer painful, because, although the famine may be over all the earth, that is to say, in the sensible part, we yet continue to have wherewith to provide for every need, which happens when the soul has no more will (of its own) for then it no longer suffers, because the will of God fully satisfies it. There is another *famine*, namely, the total privation of the very things that appear necessary: and it is not this that is here spoken of, at least with regard to Isaac; but we may take this famine for the state that comes when God wishes to drive the soul out from itself, and to cause it to be totally lost in Him. In this case it was this latter dearth which led Isaac to leave the place where he dwelt by the command of God. But where *does he go?* into a strange land; because for sometime he finds himself a *stranger* to himself. He dwells there as a pilgrim, not being permanently there, as he will be in the place that he is afterwards to possess.

God *forbids* him *to go into Egypt.* This part is most instructive for us, namely, that in the time of privations, and even of the most extreme famine, we must not sustain ourselves, nor preserve ourselves from the pain that we suffer, by multiplicity and our own efforts; but we must dwell in the place where God has placed us with much patience, until He withdraws us Himself. God, however, assures that He will be with the soul entirely abandoned to Him, in whatever place it may go to, and in whatever disposition it may be. Is not this too much for an afflicted soul, this assurance that God gives it? He again assures it that He will *give* it *the promised land*, which is the soul's permanent state in God, and is called transformation.

He will give it not only to Isaac, but to all those who, like him, will offer themselves up unreservedly to His whole will; and He even promises that there will be a great number of his descendants that will follow the same road with him. When there is said, that *all the nations of the earth will be blessed in him who will come out of Isaac,* Jesus Christ is meant, in whom all the graces and blessings are comprised.

6. *Isaac dwelt then in Gerar.*

7. *And the inhabitants of that country asked him of Rebecca: and he answered them, She is my sister.*

Isaac makes the same reply as his father did on a like occasion, by saying that *Rebecca is his sister*, and making use of this to preserve his life. Although there appears to be a falsehood here, it is nevertheless certain that he did not lie; for brother in Hebrew signifies relative, and they were accustomed to give the names of brother and sister to relatives of the nearest degrees, such as Rebecca and Isaac, who were blood-relations. Thus in the Gospel, even the relatives of our Lord are called his brethren. This conduct, which appears human, covers great mysteries. It is sometimes given to interior persons to penetrate them: and far from that obscuring the majesty of the Word of God, it serves even to make it honoured by the greatest faith.

> 8. *Abimelech, King of the Philistines, was looking out of a window, and saw Isaac sporting with Rebecca his wife;*
>
> 9. *And calling him he said to him, It is truly seen she is thy wife; wherefore saidst thou, she is my sister ?*

This charity of Abimelech in judging favourably of *Isaac*, condemns the rashness of those who censure everything immediately, and who are scandalised at the most innocent actions done in a holy freedom.

> 10. *And Abimelech charged all his people,*
>
> 11. *He that toucheth this man or his wife shall surely be put to death.*

Who will not admire God's protection of persons wholly abandoned to Him? He takes care of all their wants; He makes people take the greatest precautions for their safety, and even causes their advantages and blessings to spring from their faults. Isaac's wife, was she not more secure after the king's charge than before?

> 12. *Then Isaac sowed in that land, and received in the same year an hundred-fold; and the Lord blessed him.*
>
> 14. *This stirred up the Philistines' envy against him.*

This is the progress of the Apostolic life ; after the soul has for a long time enjoyed the repose in God Himself, it proceeds to *sow its seed*, the fruits of which do not so soon appear, but which afterwards *yields an hundred-fold*.

This *attracts the envy* of the common souls, on account of not seeing a like success to their labours ; because, working for themselves, or at least mingling something of their own interest in their most holy functions, they have not a blessing approaching that of the disinterested persons. It is God Himself who labours when we labour only for God, and if it is He who labours, how will He not bless His work?

Genesis.

15. *They stopped up all the wells which the servants of Abraham his father had digged, and filled them with earth.*

These proprietary persons persecute the Apostolic souls, *stopping up the wells* which faith, represented by *their father, had digged.* They endeavour to destroy the source of the waters they diffuse, and which has been digged by the purest faith, accusing them of evil doctrine ; for not being able to condemn their morals, they attack their faith, endeavouring *to cover it with earth,* that is to say, with things maliciously invented, which they add to their pious and solid discourse.

17. *Isaac departed thence, and came to the valley of Gerar to dwell there.*

18. *And he caused the wells to be digged again which his father Abraham had digged, and which the Philistines had filled up after his death ; and he called them by the same names which his father had given to them.*

These servants of God are often obliged to leave, and to go and *dig other wells,* which always contain the waters that faith has found, and which are always ready to water those who are so happy as to be the spiritual children of these persons who know how to dispense them. We may also observe the fidelity of Isaac in making no innovation or change in what has been established by faith, not even *the names.*

19. *They digged also in the bottom of the valley, and found there a well of springing water.*

20. *But the shepherds of Gerar strove with those of Isaac, saying, The water is ours. Wherefore he called the name of this well " Injustice."*

In the works done for God, too many people are found who *attribute* them to themselves, and who desire the glory of them as did these shepherds, who had not known that there was *springing water* in this place until Isaac had discovered it. He has no sooner found it, with much labour, than they dispute it with him, maintaining that it is theirs. But Isaac, as a perfect model of virtue, does not contest with them ; he withdraws peacefully and abandons the well to them, practising the Gospel even before the Gospel. Perfect charity is known by detachment from what is dear and useful to us ; and whoever prefers not peace to interest will lose charity for it also.

> 22. *Going from thence he digged another well, for which there was no dispute : wherefore he call it " Breadth," saying, Now the Lord has made room for me, and hath caused my goods to increase upon the earth.*

He withdraws twice for the same reason, and only takes possession of the water that no one disputes with him, because to him peaceful and tranquil waters were necessary: and as his soul had wide scope within, no more must it find anything outwardly that would limit or straiten it. The preacher of the Gospel must be thus also, above all he who preaches the most interior Gospel. He must dig his wells in places sheltered from debates and contests, and by no means quit these places until God gives the opportunity. For as his soul is at large, without anything straitening it, no more must he be under restraint in his ministry. The purity of faith and the Gospel, being drawn from God Himself, who is all peace, we must dig wells only in the places where the water is received wholly pure, and where we can possess it quietly.

> 24. *On the following night the Lord appeared to him, and said, I am the God of Abraham thy father ; fear not, for I am with thee. I will bless thee and multiply thy seed because of Abraham my servant.*

The Lord appeared unto him the night after he had found these tranquil waters : and to re-assure him still more against oppositions, *He said unto him, Fear not : I am the God of thy father, and I am with thee.* He gratified him also by this appearing, making known to him how much he approved of his practising beforehand what His son has since taught us: "And I say unto you, that ye resist not evil." We cannot forsake for God anything, however little, but He recompenses it Himself: and the more we renounce ourselves, the more He approaches us.

> 25. *He built an altar in that place, and called there upon the name of the Lord : and there he pitched his tent, and commanded his servants to dig a well.*

This Divine assurance leads these Apostolic men to offer

sacrifices to the Lord in this place of peace which they have found ; and to pitch their tent there, to dwell there, and to produce there all the fruit that God desires.

32. *The same day Isaac's servants came and told him of the success of the well which they had digged, telling him that they had found water.*

33. *Therefore he called this well "Abundance."*

God overwhelms the labour of His Apostolic workers with blessings, promising them to multiply their children of grace even to infinity on account of their faith. Thus this *well*, formed in tranquility, furnished waters in so great *abundance*, that it merited bearing this name. Whoever labours by the order of God does not fail to find in Him the source of living waters.

CHAPTER XXVII.

6. *Rebecca said to Jacob her son, I heard thy father tell Esau thy brother, saying,*

7. *Bring me something from thy hunting, and prepare it for me, that I may eat of it and bless thee before the Lord before I die.*

8. *But, my son, follow my counsel.*

9. *Go thou to the flock, and bring me two of the best goats thou canst find, that I may make savoury meat for thy father, for I know he loveth it.*

10. *And after he has eaten, he will bless thee before he dies.*

This procedure of Rebecca is so divine, that it is easy to judge from her example that a soul established in God alone, and confirmed in charity, acts by Divine inspiration even when it seems to err. God uses the affection of the mother, and the faithfulness of the son in remaining in his solitude, to execute His designs and effect His promises. According to the laws that God had established with regard to these patriarchs, everything depended on the blessing of this father; and God causes this blessing to fall quite naturally upon Jacob. There was no

lie in all this ; the truth was found there as much on the side
of nature as in the order of grace : Jacob having acquired the
natural birthright over his brother, and possessing it still more
by the pre-eminence of his interior, since he dwelt in continual
union with God, and as he was to become the father of
interior and deified souls, and God Himself was to be born of
him, he could say with truth to his father Isaac that he was
his eldest son.

11. *Jacob answered her, Thou knowest that my brother Esau
is an hairy man, and I am a smooth man.*

12. *If then my father should feel me and perceive it, I fear I
shall seem to him a deceiver, and thus I shall draw down
upon me his curse, and not his blessing.*

13. *His mother said to him, My son, upon me be this curse,
only hearken to me, and fetch me what I have told thee.*

Jacob's fear proceeded from his candour. Interior and
innocent souls fear the least turning more than death : obedience, however, re-assures them. Moreover, an interior and
truly abandoned soul, as Jacob, is contented with stating
its reasons; then it abandons itself without further reason-
ing or fearing. All persons of faith and *abandon* follow the
same conduct : so also does Providence cause everything to
succeed happily for them, even to their faults and follies. But
in this particular case of Jacob's, there was nothing but what
was most mysterious.

15. *Rebecca took Esau's best raiment, and put it upon Jacob.*

16. *And she put the skins of the kids of the goats upon his
hands and upon the smooth of his neck.*

21. *And Isaac said unto Jacob, Come near, I pray thee, that
I may feel thee my son, whether thou be my very son Esau
or not.*

22. *And Jacob went near unto Isaac his father ; and he felt
him, and said, The voice is Jacob's voice, but the hands are
the hands of Esau.*

23. *And he recognised him not.*

God *hides* these interior souls *under the skin of Esau,* that is
to say, under the appearance of the commonest life. There is

nothing on the exterior, nor on their dress, that can distinguish them; *speech* alone can make them recognised. Creatures speak as creatures, but the deified souls have only the words of God in their mouth, and they have all one and the same language. All can have the skin and raiment of Esau, but the deified souls alone can have *the voice of Jacob*. It is impossible to make these souls speak another language than that which God teaches them. They are accommodating with every one, and conform themselves easily to all that is desired according to God; but for their language, none can make them change it. It is always the same. Oh holy patriarch Isaac, how wouldst thou *know* Jacob *by the touch?* Didst thou not know indeed that the voice alone could distinguish him? But, perhaps knowing God's design, when thou recognisedst the voice of Jacob, thou sufferedst things to proceed according to the order of Providence: although we must hold to Scripture, which says, that *thou didst not know him*, God permitting it thus for the accomplishment of His designs.

27. *Isaac then blessed him and said to him,*

29. *Be lord over thy brethren, and let thy mother's sons bow down before thee. Cursed be he that curseth thee, and let every one that blesseth thee, himself be blessed.*

He gives him *authority over his brethren and the children of his mother.* It is in this that the contemplative life is truly elevated above the active life, and ought to be preferred to it, according to the witness of Jesus Christ himself given on behalf of Magdalene: " Mary, said He, " hath chosen the better part which shall not be taken away from her."

This place also truly marks how sensible God is to the cry raised by the lovers of themselves against these interior ways, and the persecutions they excite against the contemplatives: He threatens those with *His curse* who ill-treat them, and will *load* those *with His blessings,* who respect and imitate them, for there are none whose love is more purified, there are none more dear to Him; so much so that he calls them " people after His own heart," and considers them as the "apple of His eyes"; because abandoning themselves unreservedly to His whole will, they give place to Him to reign sovereignly over them.

31. *Esau presented to his father what he had prepared from his hunting, saying, Rise, my father, and eat of thy son's venison, that thou mayest give me thy blessing.*

32. *Isaac said to him, who art thou ? He answered, I am Esau thy first born.*

33. *Isaac was greatly amazed, and astonished beyond measure at what had happened ; he said, Who then is he who has already brought me what he had taken in the chase, and has given me to eat of everything before thou camest ? and behold I have blessed him and he shall be blessed.*

Isaac's astonishment was extreme. Prophets have not always the spirit of prophecy, and their natural actions serve in God's hands to accomplish His mysteries. It is, however, credible that he knew then the marvel of the secret concealed underneath, which caused his firmness in not changing what he had done, and persisting in always subjecting Esau, representing the active life, to Jacob signifying contemplation.

34. *And when Esau heard the words of his father, he cried with a great and exceeding bitter cry, and said unto his father, bless me, even me also, my father.*

35. *And he said, thy brother came with subtlety, and hath taken away thy blessing.*

Isaac does not repent even of this mistake, no more than Rebecca of this apparent fault ; for the souls that are in God cannot see anything out of God: therefore they cannot attribute anything to the creature, but, mounting higher, they make use of everything in a Divine manner. One of the surest signs that a person is truly God's, is this rare immovability of spirit in things even that cause the most confusion.

36. *And Esau said, He is rightly named Jacob, for hath he not supplanted me these two times ?*

37. *Isaac answered him, I have made him lord over thee, and all his brethren shall serve him.*

The name of *Jacob*, signifying to supplant, had been given to this patriarch on account of his having laid hold of his brother's heel in birth. Here Esau uses it to complain of his brother surprising him by artifice. It is true that Jacob takes place above him; but justly so, since it is due to him by so many titles. Notwithstanding Esau's complaints, Isaac yet continues to confirm what he had done, declaring anew that he *subjects* the active life to the contemplative. For although the active life is necessary, and has also its fruits, nevertheless it regards the contemplative as its perfection and end; since all good works tend only to the enjoyment of God, who is the portion of contemplation. Therefore it is said that *the elder shall serve the younger:* because the active life is the first that is practised: but it is as much inferior to the contemplative which follows it, as the means are inferior to the end for which they are destined.

41. *Esau always thereafter hated Jacob, because of this blessing which he had received from his father, and he said in his heart, The time of my father's death draweth nigh, and then will I slay my brother Jacob.*

42. *And when Rebecca heard this, she said to Jacob,*

43. *Believe me, my son, arise, flee thou to Laban my brother, to Haran.*

The advantage which the contemplative souls have over the active ones attracts the jealousy of the latter, who being pained at seeing them preferred, excite persecutions against them: which is the true mark that they seek themselves much in their pious labours, and not solely the interests of God.

But charity here signalises her all-heavenly prudence, by separating these two brothers on account of the difference of their ways, which can indeed agree together when they are united in one person with the subordination which God institutes for the good of many: but which harmonize with difficulty in diverse persons who go not by the same ways, because the multiplicity and bustle of the active people cannot bear the simplicity and repose of the contemplatives.

46. *Rebecca said to Isaac, I am weary of my life because of the daughters of Heth. If Jacob take to wife a daughter of this land, I have no more wish for life.*

It often happens that the active life makes an alliance with the human and sensual life. Persons unwittingly mingling prayer with activity, act usually in a very human and natural manner, and are sometimes more dangerously buried in nature than recognised sinners. Now charity, who is the mother of the active life, as well as the contemplative, *complains of this alliance,* which causes her extreme grief, and enfeebles her so greatly in the soul possessing her, that insensibly *it destroys her life.* Therefore she says : *I am weary of my life ;* as if saying, I am ready to perish in this soul because of this unhappy mixture.

But although that displeases her much, it is quite another thing when the human life is united to the contemplative : for the malignity of nature even turns into corruption the delights of the spirit, and it could not be believed how far its infection goes when it is mingled with spirituality. It is quite otherwise than in the first souls, and so much the more dangerous as it conceals itself under the most beautiful pretexts. This causes charity to say: if *Jacob* (the contemplative soul) *allies himself* with nature to produce fruit from the flesh and the spirit, which are impure fruits, *I have no more wish for life.* It is certain that the spiritual persons, who become carnal, extinguish the life of charity in a much more cruel manner than the greatest sinners and imperfect souls do. Therefore St. Paul gives this warning: " Beware that after having begun by the spirit, ye finish not by the flesh."

CHAPTER XXVIII.

1. *And Isaac called Jacob, and blessed him, and said unto him, Thou shalt not take a wife of the daughters of Canaan.*

2. *But go thou into Mesopotamia, which is in Syria, to the house of Bethuel, thy mother's father; and take a wife from one of the daughters of Laban thine uncle.*

3. *And God Almighty bless thee, and make thee fruitful and multiply thy seed, that thou mayest be the chief of many peoples.*

Isaac, *after blessing his son*—the model of the true contemplatives and souls abandoned to the conduct of their God—forbids him to ally himself with the human and carnal life, which would

I

be incompatible with his grace. He directs him on the contrary to *come out* of himself, denoted by his leaving the place where he dwells, *and to take to wife a daughter of his mother's family*, as if he said : far from making an alliance with the human or carnal life, take no other spouse than her who is connected with charity. Thou must make a new alliance with her : for although she has given thee birth, thou mightest lose her if thou didst not preserve her alliance. We must be united to pure love, and not to natural love, human or carnal. If thou actest thus, thou wilt receive a thousand blessings, and so divine a marriage will be followed by a posterity as pure as abundant.

Jacob will be in the latter ages *the father of many nations*, as he has already been in the preceding ones, with regard to all the great contemplatives who have distinguished themselves from the rest of men. But he will be so quite in another manner when this spirit will have spread over all the earth, and the world has been renewed by it. Oh God, do Thou send this interior spirit over the whole earth, and it will be created anew ! Let this same spirit rest on the waters of Thy common grace, and it will communicate to them a most abundant fruitfulness. If the interior spirit, which is but charity and prayer, animate not the faculties of our soul and their productions, they are barren in themselves, and unfruitful for others; but if this spirit of life actuates us, our works are truly worthy of God ; and the regard with which He looks upon them, causes Him to give them His blessing, by virtue of which they sanctify ourselves, and contribute to the sanctification of many others.

11. *Jacob came to a place where he wished to rest after the sun was set, and he took of the stones that were there, and put one under his head, and slept in that place.*

The soul, amorous of its God and united to him, finds nothing that hinders it from *reposing* in Him. Its journeys never interrupt its repose, nor does its repose hinder its walk. *Jacob* stops in the middle of the road, and makes his bed there. *He takes* the very *stones found there* to serve for his pillow : he chooses one of them *to support his head;* and this stone was the figure of Jesus Christ, his only support. He softly *reposes* upon this earth ; because it is the earth of repose and contemplation promised to the spiritual race, that is to say, to all the contemplative souls, who love better to repose upon this earth, though hard, than upon strange ground.

Such have always been the children of so holy a father when they have said by David: " How shall we sing the Lord's song in a strange land"? How could we rest in a multiplied way, we who are born for unity and the repose of contemplation?

Jacob *sleeps*, and enters into ecstasy *after the setting of the sun:* the excess which leads the soul into the pure divine light, is only caused by the extinction of natural light; and it is necessary that what is acquired give place to what is to be infused.

12. *And he saw in a dream a ladder, whose foot rested upon the earth, and the top of which reached to heaven: and angels of God were ascending and descending by this ladder.*

13. *He also saw the Lord resting upon the top of the ladder, who said to him, I am the Lord, the God of Abraham thy father, and the God of Isaac. To thee and to thy seed also will I give the land on which thou sleepest.*

Jacob, sleeping in a mystic sleep, *sees a ladder going from this earth* of repose *up to heaven; and God resting upon the top of the ladder.* This ladder, resting with its foot upon this earth of repose, and which served at the other end for repose to God Himself, marks the degrees that must be ascended in order to proceed from the repose of contemplation up to the repose in God alone. The distance is great. These souls, although wholly *angelic, ascend and descend:* for even the degrees of ascent often become for them degrees of descent, either apparent or real: but everything is equal for such a soul by the excellent use it knows to make of them,—abandoning to God everything that regards it. *The top* of this ladder *is in heaven* and in God Himself; since Scripture says, that God rested upon the top of the ladder. This means, that these steps, representing the ways of ascent and descent variously conducting to God, all cease when one is arrived at Him alone, just as a ladder would be useless to a person who by its aid had ascended to where it reached.

The Lord was resting upon the ladder. He who supports the whole world, and sustains it by His almighty arm, can He lean upon anything? Yes, truly; for He finds a delicious repose in souls who, by their perfect annihilation, by the loss of all means, have arrived at the last degree of their origin, which is God.

With what complacency would God not repose in a soul which reposes no more but in Him ? This is to repose in Himself, since this soul has no longer anything out of Him.

This mysterious *ladder* also teaches us by God resting upon its summit, that as souls having come out from Him by the creation, come by these steps of descent upon the earth of an impure life ; so also to return into Him, they must re-ascend by the way they have descended. This thought has caused many mystics to say, that the soul, to re-enter into God by a perfect union, must have attained to the purity of its creation ; which is understood by the loss of all spot and propriety. This is very well expressed by this ladder, where to arrive at God, the same degree must be attained which was left in descending from Him,—which is quite natural.

It was here God promised that *this land* of repose *would be given* not only to these first mystics, but also *to all their descendants;* and that all the persons who would walk in this same way, and who like Jacob would rest in contemplation, would be able to ascend the whole ladder and arrive at God. Therefore the Lord said to Jacob : *They will possess the land on which thou liest*; for this was the place whereon the ladder was set : otherwise, the promise would have been a small affair taken in the strict letter, since he could rest only on a very small piece of ground.

14. *Thy seed shall be multiplied as the dust of the earth. Thou shalt spread abroad from the east to the west, and from the north to the south, and all nations of the earth shall be blessed in thee, and in him that will come out of thee.*

He promises him that this interior people will become so *numerous that it will equal the dust of the earth.* This expression, the dust of the earth, can be understood as to number, or as to the quality of this people. According to number, God represents to him that it will be so multiplied, that some of them will be found in all places, and that in all nations there will be this interior people ; which has been indeed verified, and is and will always be true : for there is no place where some are not found. According to quality, they are souls so annihilated that they are reduced into the dust of their nothingness ; therefore Scripture says not : they will be multiplied as much as the dust, or more : for that would signify but the excess of number; but it says, as the dust, expressing very well their annihilation.

> 15. *I will be thy protector wherever thou goest; I will bring thee again into this land, and will not leave thee until I have fulfilled all that I have said unto thee.*

God assures him that He Himself will *protect him*, and *bring him back*: showing by this that it is He who conducts souls abandoned to Him, in all ways, until He brings them back into Himself, their birth-place.

> 16. *And Jacob awaked out of his sleep, and he said, Surely the Lord is in this place and I knew it not!*

When he *awoke from his mystic sleep, he said that God was there and he knew it not;* not that he didn't know that God was everywhere; but because the souls of this degree are so absorbed in peace and union, and faith conducts them so nakedly, that they possess God without thinking they possess Him, and without having any knowledge of it, with the exception of some moments, when He makes Himself a little perceived, which is as when one awakens from a deep sleep. Faith and *abandon* blind them, as the too great light of the sun dazzles, so that they cannot distinguish anything of Him. It is as a person seeing in the atmosphere and breathing it without thinking that he sees it and breathes it, on account of his not reflecting upon it. These souls, although wholly penetrated by God, do not think of it, for God hides from them what they are; therefore is this way called *mystic*, meaning secret and imperceptible.

> 17. *And he was seized with fright, and cried, How terrible is this place! Surely this can be no other than the house of God, and the gate of heaven.*

Scripture says *that he was afraid, and cried, How terrible is this place!* This followed on the knowledge given him of the extreme sufferings through which these chosen souls must pass to arrive at the gate of heaven: for otherwise, what was there dreadful in this gate, and should he not sooner have entered into admiration and transports of joy, discovering the abode of glory? Yet, on the contrary, he cries, How terrible and dreadful is this place! This can be nothing less than the house of God and the gate of heaven. Should he not rather have said in the usual manner: Oh how desirable this place is! How lovely and charming it is, since it is the house of God and the gate of heaven? But as at this moment he comprehended more than he was to express, he was contented to say that. He knew all that he must suffer, and the strange ways through which God conducts souls to bring them to the gate of heaven; but he said no more, because there are secrets of which it is not permitted for man to speak.

18. *And Jacob rose up early in the morning, and took the stone that he had put for his pillow, and set it up for a monument, and poured oil upon the top of it.*

20. *And he made a vow, saying, If God remain with me and lead me in the road that I go, and give me bread to eat, and raiment to put on;*

21. *And if I return to my father's house in peace, the Lord shall be my God;*

22. *And this stone which I have set up for a monument shall be called the house of God.*

This *monument* was to be a memorial to posterity of what had happened to Jacob in this place, and what he had there known.

It is the property of the knowledge we receive in this so obscure a way, to cause fear and hesitation. Moreover, in the way of faith and abandon, we should stop neither at visions, words, favours nor anything assuring, for this assurance would retard the course: therefore Jacob, well instructed both for himself and for us, without stopping at what he had seen, or even what God had said to him, and courageously going beyond all things to halt only at the divine moment of providence, who is the only assurance without assurance of abandoned souls, says to himself: *If the Lord remain with me, and if* by His providence *He conducts me,* so that He protect me from sin *in* so dangerous and intricate a way; then shall I confess Him as my God. But although I blindly abandon myself to His providence, and desire no other conduct than His during all the way, yet cannot I have complete assurance and experience that He is my God, until I be in the peace of *my father's house,* that is to say, in the repose of my origin, because the obscurity of this way would always keep me in some inequality.

But how can a *stone* be called the *house of God?* It is because the stone being the sign of the mystic repose, where everything is hidden, the soul which, by a rare felicity has passed over all the mystic deserts and has arrived in God Himself, cries for itself and others that the mystic way is assuredly the habitation of God.

CHAPTER XXIX.

9. *And while Jacob yet spake with the shepherds, Rachel came with her father's sheep; for she tended the flock herself.*

10. *And when Jacob saw Rachel, the daughter of Laban, his mother's brother, and the sheep of Laban, he rolled the stone from the well's mouth, and watered the flock.*

It is here *Jacob*, who *gives water* for the use of *Rachel;* and it was Rebecca who gave it for the servants and camels of Isaac. This difference marks for us a profound mystery: neither Jacob nor Rachel, at the time the water was poured out, was yet sufficiently prepared for the spiritual marriage: Rachel had yet no tincture of the spiritual life; therefore Jacob himself must make the waters flow, for it is to him, on account of his father, that the promise had been made. Moreover, Rachel was to be barren; and although she contributed with Jacob to the birth of two numerous enough tribes, yet the source of living water, Jesus Christ, was not to issue from her, but from Jacob, who, for this reason, gives the water—the figure of the graces of salvation and perfection which were to be communicated by the Saviour of the world. But Rebecca, being a source whence was to issue the pure and vivifying water, which is Jesus Christ, could water the peoples in the person of Eliezer and on behalf of Isaac. Jacob performs the office of shepherd to Rachel, for he is in Jesus Christ, or rather Jesus Christ is in him, the legitimate Shepherd, who is to water his flock with the water from the rock.

11. *And Jacob kissed Rachel, and lifted up his voice and wept.*

He *kisses her* as a sign of the union he makes with her, associating her by this kiss to the way and life of faith. He *sheds tears* on account of the presentiment he has that although she is most beautiful and extremely virtuous, yet she will never have the advantage of producing Jesus Christ in souls : the love that Jacob bore for her, being mixed with the natural, could alone hinder this production, which shows that a greater purity and more complete stripping is necessary for the Apostolic life, than for every other life however holy it may be, and although it appear full of virtues.

20. *Jacob served Laban seven years for Rachel; and this time seemed to him only a few days, so great was his love for her.*

The natural love that Jacob bore *for Rachel* was a weakness which God permitted in this holy patriarch : so the *seven years that he served* in the hope of espousing her were not counted, and *they appeared but a few days.* But these kinds of weaknesses in souls of this fortitude serve also the design of God, contributing to their annihilation, so as to render them fit for the cross, and at the same time to dispose them for the Apostolic life, which is given by the cross, represented by Leah. The sweetnesses of contemplation alone (denoted by Rachel) can never produce this life divinely fruitful on behalf of souls. It must be the cross that gives it. Prayer must be joined to the cross in order to bear these fruits of grace : the cross pours out the blood of Jesus Christ into the womb of prayer so as to render it fruitful ; and prayer sheds upon our crosses the Spirit of God, whom it attracts from heaven to sanctify them.

21. *After that he said unto Laban, Give me my wife, for the time has arrived when I must espouse her.*
22. *Laban got ready the marriage feast.*
23. *And in the evening he took Leah his daughter into Jacob's chamber.*

God, who is full of goodness, agreeably deceives us. He first makes us love interior sweetnesses, and then when we think of attaching ourselves to them and of living contented with them, He substitutes the cross in their place. Interior consolations (figured by Rachel) being always agreeable, the soul through infidelity and feebleness becomes attached to them in a disorderly manner. God, however, suffers it to love them for a time, and bestows them abundantly : but it is to dispose it to suffer the cross He prepares for it.

24. *Jacob found in the morning that it was Leah.*

25. *And he said to his father-in-law, How hast thou treated me thus? Have I not served thee for Rachel? Why hast thou deceived me?*

By day it is Rachel we love, that is to say, whilst the illuminative state lasts: *by night* it is Leah we possess, when the obscurity of faith has arrived. Faith loves Leah because of her fruitfulness : nature loves Rachel because of her beauty. Leah is blear-eyed ; but she is as agreeable in the repose of the night as Rachel ; she is even taken for her. The cross is ugly when it is regarded with reflection, but the soul that possesses it in the repose of union without reflecting upon it, finds there as many pleasures as amidst the greatest sweetnesses. Self-love, then, which served God for sweetnesses, and expected to possess them for ever, finding nothing else but distaste and the cross, complains of it to God Himself. What, it says, is this the reward Thou hast promised me for my long services? I believed that afterwards Thou wouldst load me with spiritual pleasures : and behold Thou sendest me only afflictions and bitterness ! Whence comes to me this so unlooked for change?

26. *Laban answered him, It is not the custom of this country to give the youngest daughters before the first-born.*

27. *Pass the week with her, and I will give thee the other afterwards for the time of seven other years which thou wilt serve me.*

28. *Jacob accepted her ; and after seven days he espoused Rachel.*

God, full of compassion for this soul, consoles it and says to it : Suffer only for some days the afflictions that I apportion to thee : and afterwards will I give thee in real and intimate possession the sweetnesses which thou hast only outwardly and for some moments. But grief must precede this pleasure ; for the cross in My sight possesses the *birth-right* and it must pass before the intimate and lasting pleasures; for all the enjoyment of this life is a very little thing, and I grant it to thee only on account of thy weakness; but after thou shalt have tasted of this eternal sweetness, which I promised thee, thou must yet *serve me seven years,* so as to repay with some labours a good that cannot be estimated.

30. *Jacob having at last obtained the so much desired nuptials, preferred the love of the second to the first, and served Laban yet seven other years.*

Souls not advanced in the ways of truth prefer the love of delights to the love of the cross : and this is what greatly retards their progress. God permits all this in Jacob to instruct us : since as the great Apostle declares, "There is nothing in Scripture that is not written for our instruction."

31. *When the Lord saw that Leah was little esteemed, He opened her womb, whilst her sister remained barren.*
32. *She conceived, and bare a son whom she called Reuben, saying, The Lord hath looked upon my humiliation, and now my husband will love me.*

The cross, so little agreeable and so little loved, is always *fruitful:* which makes an enlightend soul prefer it above everything else ; but sweetnesses, which cause only an apparent pleasure, have a veritable *barrenness,* whilst the cross, under the form of bitterness preserves inexpressible advantages.

The cross, represented by *Leah,* expresses the joy she has of being a mother, in the hope that *her husband,* the soul to whom she is united, seeing her fruitfulness, will entertain for her all the esteem that is due to her.   Nevertheless, she is not carried away by it, recognising that all comes from God, who has given her this advantage so as to raise her from her natural *abjection,* and faithfully consecrating to Him all the glory of it.   The cross must be judged by its fruits : the senses cannot taste them, but the spirit discovers them by faith.

34. *She conceived again.*
35. *And the third time she bare a son, and she said, Now will my husband be more united to me, seeing I have given him three sons ; therefore she called his name Levi.*

It is a strange thing that the cross, which has so many

advantages, has so much difficulty in making herself loved. Behold her here producing the priestly race and all that there is of the greatest: yet hardly can she make herself loved. The first time she gives birth she aspires to nothing but to render herself less despicable : at the second, she hopes to render herself worthy of being loved : but the third time, after producing Levi, who is the Royal Priest, she believes she has made herself to be desired, and that the ˉul to whom she has been given, having become wiser, will long to be united to her.

> 36. *She conceived again for the fourth time, and she bare a son and said, Now will I praise the Lord : therefore she called him Judah, and left off bearing.*

But, *at the fourth time,* she only *gives praises to the Lord,* which is to announce *Jesus Christ* in *Judah,* from whom he was to proceed. And as in Jesus Christ there is found the end and consummation of every desire ; so after having given Judah *she left off bearing.*

The cross, enraptured at so noble a production, which she sees born from her, holds herself so high above everything created, that she speaks no more of Jacob, and shows no more desire to possess him, as at the other times ; but only with a bold flight at the sight of so admirable a production, she cries: Oh, this time *I will praise the Lord,* having nothing more upon the earth that can arrest my desire ! The cross could not produce anything greater than the salvation of all the world, which she has truly given birth to, when, by the blood which Jesus Christ has shed upon the cross, peace has been made between things in heaven and things on the earth.

CHAPTER XXX.

> 1. *And when Rachel saw that she was barren, she envied her sister; and said unto Jacob, Give me children or else I die.*
>
> 2. *And Jacob's anger was raised; and he said to her, Am I God, who hath withheld from thee the fruit of the womb?*

Sweetnesses, although spiritual, would desire to have the

advantage of the cross ; and tiring of their barrenness, they say to the soul which possesses them : *Cause some production to be born* of us, *else we die;* why should the cross have all the advantage? They would wish either to exist no longer, or to participate in the fruitfulness of the cross. The soul, seeing the little solidity of this way of sweetnesses, grows angry, and shows it that *God* alone can *make it fruitful.* The cross and consolation are trials which exercise differently the same person, just as these two wives, who were the figure of them, exercise Jacob their husband. To be faithful in these trials, we must receive them equally from *God's hand,* and regard them only in Him.

3. *And she said, Behold my maid Bilhah, go in unto her ; and she shall bear upon my knees, that I may also have children by her.*

4. *And she gave him Bilhah her handmaid to wife.*

5. *And Bilhah conceived, and bare Jacob a son.*

Rachel, seeing that she cannot produce anything on account of her barrenness, has recourse *to her servant.* So the soul in the sweetness of contemplation, seeing herself powerless, has often recourse to a servant by whom to obtain productions, making use of some exterior works of charity, which she appropriates to console herself for her barrenness, and to provide for herself a natural support.

14. *And one day Reuben went into the field in the days of wheat harvest, and found mandrakes, which he brought to Leah his mother. Rachel said to her, Give me of thy son's mandrakes.*

15. *Leah replied; Is it not sufficient for thee to have taken away my husband without desiring also to have my son's mandrakes? Rachel answered, I am willing that he sleep with thee this night, provided thou givest me of these mandrakes.*

The whole illuminative life is yet but a life of infancy and feebleness, considering the life of faith which is to follow it. Rachel is so childish that she prefers the pleasure of seeing and smelling *mandrakes,* plants beautiful to the sight, and of an excellent odour, to the real possession of her husband. Effeminate souls full of sensual inclinations resemble her in that: they prefer the sweet to the solid, which is the possession of God in Himself above all gifts.

16. *And when Jacob returned from the field in the evening, Leah went out to meet him, and said to him, Thou must come with me, for I have purchased this favour by giving my sister my son's mandrakes.*

17. *And God heard her prayers; she conceived and bare a son for the fifth time.*

The strong and generous souls who have been rendered such by the cross, willingly give up all delights and everything that is from without, for the real possession of the spouse, as did Leah: so God blessed so just a choice by a new fruitfulness, giving her yet two sons and one daughter. This marks also how the soul which has abandoned all for God, *runs* with pleasure *to tell Him* that she merits *possessing Him, having acquired it* by the destitution of all gifts.

22. *The Lord also remembered Rachel, and hearkened to her, and made her fruitful.*

23. *She conceived and bare a son; and she said, The Lord hath taken away my reproach.*

God, whose goodness is infinite, and who leaves nothing without recompense, treats the feeble souls according to their feebleness. He had pity upon Rachel, *and made her a mother.* This teaches us that these souls of graces and sensible favour having become riper towards the end of their career, bear some fruit; but it approaches neither in quantity nor quality to that produced by the souls who have been conducted by a way as mighty as it has been crucified. Then they are extremely rejoiced at this production, and say that God has raised them from their lowliness.

25. *And when Joseph was born, Jacob said to his father-in-law, Let me go now, that I may return to my country and my own land.*

The way of lights and sweetnesses has no sooner become fruitful, and outwardly produces some mark of its beauty, than the soul, all enraptured to see such beautiful fruits, because they retain the beauty of their mother, earnestly desires to come forth from this first way to introduce them into that of *abandon.* Therefore *Jacob presses Laban to allow him to go :* as if he apprehended that his children might contract something foreign by a longer sojourn in this land, which would be a dangerous mixture.

CHAPTER XXXI.

3. *And the Lord said unto Jacob, Return unto the land of thy fathers, and to thy kindred, and I will be with thee.*

God, who had a particular care over Jacob, and who with paternal attention kept him under the conduct of His providence, Himself bids him *return to the land of his fathers :* this is lest he should be tempted to enter into other ways on account of his great riches. He promises him a second time *that He will be with him* in all his labours until He has conducted him to his origin and to the place of repose in God. Until that time some change is always to be feared.

8. *The lambs of various colours were the reward of Jacob.*

Jacob's sheep were of various colours ; to teach us, that until the soul has permanently arrived in God, there is always some change in it, and it varies incessantly, being sometimes in one state, sometimes in another ; sometimes in peace, at other times in trouble and agitation. It is only the state of the soul in God which varies no more : for it has come to the purity and simplicity of its origin.

13. *I am the God who appeared unto thee at Bethel, where thou anointedst the stone, and where thou madest a vow. Get thee out speedily from this land, and return to the land of thy birth.*

Remember, says the Lord, *the stone* where thou *madest a vow. unto me,* and where I promised to conduct thee. It is there I wish to lead thee back, for that is thy birth-place, where I desire to reconduct thee so as to lose thee in Me, and make thee flow again into the source whence thou art sprung.

> 18. *Jacob took all that he had acquired in Mesopotamia, and went on his way.*
>
> 19. *And when Laban had gone to shear his sheep, Rachel stole her father's idols.*

Jacob took everything that was his, and left nothing ; but it is easy to see from *the theft of Rachel,* how far removed the souls of lights are from the perfect stripping of those conducted by crosses. The former have always some idols or attachments which they carry with them, which the others have not. Leah takes nothing but her children, and God suffices her for everything.

> 22. *And it was told Laban on the third day that Jacob was fled.*
>
> 23. *And immediately he pursued him for seven days, and overtook him at Mount Gilead.*
>
> 24. *But God appeared to Laban in a dream, and said to him, Take heed that thou speak not harshly to Jacob.*

Who will not admire the care God takes of souls abandoned to Him. He prevents on their behalf even the least accidents, not sparing even *revelations* or miracles to protect them from the ill-treatment of their persecutors, as is seen here by the admirable manner in which God delivered Jacob and all his family from the anger of Laban.

> 37. *Jacob said to Laban:*
>
> 38. *Thy sheep and thy she-goats have not been barren, and the rams of thy flock have I not eaten.*
>
> 39. *That which was torn of beasts I brought not unto thee ; I bare the loss of it ; and thou didst require of me all that was stolen.*
>
> 40. *The heat of the day consumed me, and the frost by night, and sleep fled mine eyes.*
>
> 41. *Thus have I served thee in thy house these twenty years.*

Behold the qualities of the good shepherd, who does no hurt

to the flock, who suffers nothing to be taken by the enemy; who exposes himself for the sheep, and who gives his life for them; who burdens himself with all their interests, and who takes upon himself all the hurt that can be done them. There will not easily be found in all Scripture a figure more full of the Shepherd JESUS, than that seen in Jacob; nor of the qualities that all true shepherds ought to possess. But let no one flatter himself he is able fully to perform all these great duties if he is not like Jacob, strong in God by a profound interior.

CHAPTER XXXII.

1. *And Jacob went on his way, and the angels of God met him.*

This consolation given by *the angels*, is to prepare the soul for great combats it must sustain before entering into God. It is no longer the persecution of the creatures it is to apprehend, it is God Himself; but first must be sustained the attack of earthly enemies, who are only the forerunners of another combat, which is not feared, because not known : a visible combat is feared which is only apparent; and a real combat is not feared, because it is unknown.

6. *Esau, thy brother cometh to meet thee, and four hundred men with him.*

7. *Then Jacob was greatly afraid and distressed.*

We often distress ourselves about an imaginary evil, whilst we remain firm and constant in real combats : thus *Jacob fears* extremely *the meeting with Esau*, who nevertheless will do him no evil; but he does not yet dread many other combats which God prepares for him, although by His particular assistance he is to come out happily from them.

9. *Jacob prayed to God thus: God of my father Abraham, God of my father Isaac, Lord which said unto me, Return into thy country, and to thy birth-place, and I will bless thee.*

348

10. *I am unworthy of all thy mercies, and of the truth which thou hast manifested in the fulfilment of the promises thou didst make to thy servant. I crossed this river of Jordan having but my staff, and now I return with two bands.*

The manner in which Jacob returns to God in his affliction shows how useful pain and affliction are. They bring God's favours to remembrance ; not only to serve for some consolation, but also to redouble confidence. Jacob represents to God all *His promises:* he does not complain : he lays before Him only all the blessings He has bestowed on him, pleading that they may not be rendered useless.

He asks of Him His help in a manner so powerful and so tender, that the words related in the text express it more than all we can say of it. The perplexity and grief in which he finds himself well represent a soul returning by the way of faith and *abandon* into God its origin : for then it is in doubts and pains ; the fear of death seizes upon it, it appears to it inevitable. But what death does it fear ? The death caused by sin. It knows that it has often been victorious over this enemy, whom it has ruled and supplanted ; but seeing itself about to fall into his hands, it does not doubt but that he will avenge himself : and being assured that he will not spare it, it seems to have no power to evade its loss. Then this poor soul, pressed on all sides, reminds God that it is He who has made it enter upon this way, and that it is to blindly obey Him that it has bound itself to it ; that it has wholly abandoned itself to Him ; after which it prays Him to protect it. It represents to Him also that its *fathers* have walked by the same way, and that it is on that account He has declared Himself their God. It humbles itself before Him, and puts Him in mind of His *truth.*

11. *Deliver me from the hand of my brother Esau, for I fear him exceedingly, lest he smite the mother with the children.*

12. *Thou hast promised to bless me with riches, and to multiply my seed as the sand of the sea, which cannot be numbered.*

It is a beautiful expression, *to smite the mother with the children.* Sin smites *the mother*—righteousness acquired by grace; and also *the children,* the virtues and good works. Now this soul pressed with anguish sees itself on the eve of losing both. It forgets all the other goods, and thinks only of its own righteousness, which it sees itself on the point of losing : it freely gives up the other goods, that is to say, it consents to the loss of heavenly inclinations and favours. It is just that all that be ravished from it by sin, which here appears inevitable to it; but its very integrity and its fruits—the divine virtues, ah! this is what it cannot consent to lose. No, poor afflicted soul, thou wilt have more fear than hurt: there is nothing for thee to be afraid of; for God will prevent the disaster thou art threatened with.

13. *Jacob passed the night in that place; and he put aside out of all he had, what he had designed to be offered to his brother Esau.*

23. *And he sent over the brook all that he possessed.*

24. *He remained alone in that place. And there appeared at the same time a man, who wrestled with him until the morning.*

25. *And when he saw that he could not prevail against Jacob, he touched the sinew of his thigh, and it shrank immediately.*

Jacob, as I have said, hazards all his goods and *remains alone.* Oh poor man, you think you have only to fight an enemy that you can even appease by your presents; you have already escaped the pursuit of your father-in-law (signifying the creature); you think, according to your own judgment, to elude likewise the other enemies: but you do not know you must combat God Himself, and that it is He who comes to attack you. Now this combat is the last and most severe of all. To maintain a combat against God, to sustain the weight of God's strength, is a thing that experience alone can make understood. It always costs something this war, as to Jacob, who became lame by it.

26. *This man said to him, Let me go, for the day breaketh. Jacob replied, I will not let thee go until thou hast blessed me.*

27. *And he said unto him, What is thy name? And he said, Jacob.*

28. *The man said to him, Until now thou hast been called Jacob, but hereafter thou shall be called Israel; for if thou hast been mighty against God, how much more so wilt thou be against men.*

This combat being the last of all, after having borne it, *the name must be changed*, and the new name is given, as to Abraham and Sarah. This is clear in the Old and New Testaments. But this soul here loses its own righteousness, and its own strength, to be invested with the strength of God: thus this name of Israel given him, signifies *mighty against God*, as if it was said, strong as God, and with the strength of God Himself. For this reason all Jacob's children and his people, who are to be God's spiritual people, are to be called the people of Israel, clothed with the strength of God Himself: thus it is said to this people in Exodus: "The Lord shall fight for you, and ye shall hold your peace," meaning, that He Himself fights in them, and that they have but to keep themselves at rest. And in the book of Samuel: "Thou comest to me with a sword, and with a spear, and with a shield: but I come to thee in the name of the Lord of Hosts." This soul, then, clad with the strength of God, no longer fears either men or demons: for having borne the combat with the very God, what is there more to fear?

31. *As soon as Jacob had passed this place, which he had called Penuel, he saw the Sun rising; but he was lame of one leg.*

After these terrible combats *the Sun rises:* the creature being still further destroyed and drained off, melted and annihilated, comprehends more truly what God is, true *Sun* of all beings, although it can still less comprehend Him, the excess of its absorption into Him rendering Him still more incomprehensible to it, although it knows Him better than it ever did. These persons, happy enough to have sustained with faithfulness the Divine Combat, may appear to the eyes of the creatures still more feeble than they were formerly believed to be, but in truth they never were stronger, since by the loss of their own strength they have entered into the strength of God; thus Jacob, although become lame, bears the name and fulfils the meaning of Israel—*mighty against God.*

CHAPTER XXXIII.

10. *Jacob said to Esau his brother, I have seen thy face this day, as though I had seen the face of God. Be then favourable to me.*

11. *Take this present which I have offered to thee, and which I have received from God, who gives all things.*

When the new name has been given, and the soul is well advanced, *it sees* all things in *God* and *God* in all things. Sin, which before gave it so much fright, terrifies it no longer ; all hell itself could not dismay it, because it can no longer see anything distinct from God Himself, where there is no sin, but perfect Holiness. This manner of expressing itself, so simple and natural, is so appropriate to the soul of this degree, that although it would, it could not do otherwise. Let those who do not comprehend this believe it not impossible. It must be thus, because the soul that has been received into God can no longer see these things but as God sees them, without fear, without trouble, without emotion, without malice, without fault, taking part in His Divine Attributes in proportion as it is received into His Unity. Jacob shows also to Esau that everything which he gives him is from God, because it is He who gives all things. It is the property of those persons established in the Divine Truth to attribute nothing to themselves, but to refer all to God.

CHAPTER XXXV.

1. *And God said unto Jacob, Get thee up quickly unto Bethel, and dwell there, and there build an altar unto the Lord who appeared to thee when thou fleddest from thy brother Esau.*

2. *Then Jacob, having gathered together all his household, said unto them, Cast out from you the strange gods that are in the midst of you ; purify yourselves, and change your garments.*

God bids the soul, after so many fatigues and combats sustained on the road, *go* to the place of its origin, where He conducts it with so much goodness by His admirable providence, *and build there an altar.* But before the superior part of the soul is received into God, it must have attained to the purity of its creation ; and for this state all propriety must be taken away,

and all faults and spots cut off from the inferior parts, represented by *Jacob's family.*

It is necessary that everything be extremely *clean,* and *have
changed garments,* and have become quite different by renova-
tion.   Jacob does nothing for himself in preparing for so
great a good : for it was solely the work of God who had conducted him by this road, and who was bringing him back to his
origin ; but he commands the inferior part to *leave* everything
strange and proper to itself, so that nothing may further retard
this happy loss into God.

Let us remark, too, that in so holy a family as Jacob's, there
are still found some *idols;* and perhaps some of his servants
were idolaters.   What place is there so holy, what soul so pure,
in which there is not mixed some impurity ?

> 3. *Let us arise, and go up to Bethel, and there build an altar
> unto God, who hath heard me in the day of my affliction,
> and who hath been with me on my way.*

> 7. *And he built there an altar, and called the place the House
> of God, for there God had appeared unto him when he
> fled from Esau his brother.*

Then the soul is apprised of God's faithfulness, and it knows
how *He has conducted it.*   Then it is delivered from the true
afflictions and pains of the spirit, and from all inquietude,
although it is still reserved for good crosses ; but these will be
crosses it will bear like Jesus Christ and with him, and which
it can bear in all security.

It is the property of this soul to render back everything to
God in the same place, and in the very manner He has given
it.   Then there is made the pure sacrifice, which is favourably
received.

> 9. *God appeared unto Jacob the second time,*

> 10. *And said to him, Until now thou hast been called Jacob,
> but hereafter shall thy name be Israel.*

> 13. *And God withdrew from him.*

God again blesses Jacob, and confirms to him his new *name.*
The state is given to the soul a long time before it is confirmed
in it.   We have for a long time the transitory dispositions ;
then the state is given ; but confirmation in the state is a much

later thing, and a much more eminent grace. Confirmation is here given to Jacob when God repeats to him so positively, *thy name shall be Israel.*

It is added that God *withdrew*, or disappeared, from Jacob's eyes. This signifies how God, having raised the creature's capacity in order to elevate it up to Himself, lowers Himself also towards it without ceasing to be what He is ; but this is only to take it, carry it away, and lose it into Himself, disappearing so much the more from the eyes of the spirit as He causes it to be lost in Himself.

16. *And setting out from that place, he came in the spring time to the road leading to Ephrath, where Rachel travailed.*

18. *And feeling that death was coming upon her by reason of the violence of her pain, being ready to expire, she called her son's name Benoni, that is to say, son of my grief : but his father called him Benjamin, that is to say, son of my right hand.*

19. *Thus died Rachel, and she was buried in the way to Ephrath, since called Bethlehem.*

The soul confirmed in God is entirely separated from all natural and spiritual feelings ; should there remain ever so little, God makes them *die* as He did Rachel. Scripture does not say that Jacob wept for her : for being then well established in the will of God, he could not be afflicted at this loss, which he saw in God Himself to be advantageous for him. For this is a light of this state, which shows that God does everything for our advantage, and that everything contributes to our greatest good. Behold, then, this soul deprived of everything it had dear to it in nature ; there remains nothing to it but God alone and the cross ; but the cross is no longer painful to it ; it has known its value too well not to esteem it ; and it is too strong in God to have any difficulty in bearing it. There remains, however, a secret love for Rachel's productions, because they are sweet and amiable, and those of the cross are somewhat wilder. Moreover, the fruits of sweetness and union contain within themselves their beauty, and they show outwardly all that they are ; but the fruits of the cross are bitter at first; they are only sweet and admirable in their continuations, for they terminate at nothing less than the production of Jesus Christ.

CHAPTER XXXVI.

6. *And Esau took his wives, and his sons, and his daughters, and all the persons of his house, and his cattle, and all his beasts, and all his substance which he had got in the land of Canaan, and went into the country from the face of his brother Jacob.*

15. *The sons of Esau were Princes, Prince Teman, Prince Omar.*

Who can sufficiently admire how God conducts things by the wisdom of His providence? The child of wrath *separates himself* from the chosen of God, the nation of the flesh removes itself from the generation of the spirit, and the active way is divided from the contemplative. *Esau goes into another country,* leaving the chosen nation in peaceful possession of the region of repose.

But Esau was at once great upon the earth; people spoke of him only. As for Israel, he remains little in the eyes of men and great before God; he has only the cross, which will follow him even to the tomb, and by which he will triumph in Jesus Christ.

CHAPTER XXXVII.

3. *Now Israel loved Joseph more than all his children, because he was the son of his old age; and he made him a coat of many colours.*

4. *And when his brethren saw that their father loved him more than all his brethren, they hated him, and could not speak peaceably unto him.*

The history of Joseph is a living expression of a predestined soul; and the various incidents related of him in the sacred text admirably mark the various states through which one of the most chosen souls must pass in order to arrive at the perfection destined for it. God makes it first pass through a state of spiritual *infancy*, in which it receives only sweetness and caresses. It seems as if God was occupied only in decorating and embellishing it and neglecting the others. This attracts, indeed, the jealousy of other persons, who see that all the favours are for it. But how dearly they will be sold to it !

> 9. *Joseph related to his brethren also another dream which he had : It seemed to me in my dream that the sun and moon and eleven stars worshipped me.*

God Himself makes known to it by *dreams* and visions something of its future elevations ; and this simple and innocent soul *tells it to its* spiritual *brothers*, but who are far removed from simplicity. Thus do they attribute to pride and idle fancy what comes from the Holy Spirit.

> 17. *And Joseph went after his brethren, and found them in Dothan.*
>
> 18. *When they perceived him afar off, before he came to them, they resolved to kill him.*
>
> 19. *And they said one to another, Behold this dreamer cometh.*
>
> 20. *Let us go and slay him, and then we shall see what his dreams will be worth to him.*

Amongst jealous brethren there are found some who, having strayed from the way of truth, take everything amiss, and who, pretending to punish a crime, which exists only in their imagination, wish to *take the life* of an innocent person. Such are these false zealots, who, in order to extinguish interior ways, accuse those who teach and maintain them of pretended crimes, designing thereby to *destroy the life*, if not of the body, at least of the spirit and reputation.

> 21. *Reuben, hearing them speak thus, endeavoured to deliver him out of their hands, and he said to them,*
>
> 22. *Slay him not, and shed not his blood, but cast him into this pit in the desert, and preserve your hands pure.*

The sweetnesses of spiritual infancy are hardly passed than the strangest crosses are prepared. We see ourselves exposed to the most extreme persecutions. Joseph is as a sheep amid a pack of wolves; but God, who continually takes care of souls who give themselves to Him without reserve, finds some defender to draw them from the hands of their enemies.

> 23. *And immediately when Joseph had come to his brethren, they stript him of his robe of many colours which covered him,*
>
> 24. *And cast him into this old pit, where there was no water.*
>
> 26. *And Judah said unto his brethren, What profit is it if we slay our brother, and conceal his blood ?*
>
> 27. *Come, and let us sell him unto the Ishmaelites, and let not our hand be upon him, for he is our brother and our flesh. And his brothers were content.*

This poor lamb suffers himself to be *stripped*. It is thus also with souls destined to a great interior. The first stripping is performed in them by the privation of gifts and sensible graces, represented by their *coat of many colours*. The soul, seeing these things taken away from it, believes, from this first stripping, that it has come to its end, and that it is going to lose its life. It would, indeed, be thus if God gave the power to its enemies.

This soul, conducted by *abandon*, allows everything to be done to it, without saying anything or complaining ; it seeks, however, on every side for some help to come to it, as did the prophet king when in this state he said, *I have lifted up mine eyes to the mountains to look whence my help will come.* Then he adds, filled with truth, *My help can only come from the Lord, who has made heaven and earth.* There is no other help for the soul but the Lion of the tribe of Judah, who delivers it from the approaching death to make it endure a thousand and a thousand deaths. Oh, my God, it is thus that Thou deliverest Thy dearest friends! Thou retardest their death to make them suffer an infinity of deaths. Every day feeling the rigours of death makes persecuted persons take courage in bewailing their distresses ; and when they believe he is going to impart to them of his sweets, which is the loss of this life, he removes himself from them. It is a continual game of death's to show himself to those persons and to hide himself from them. St. Paul has expressed it for all when he said, *Through all our life we cease not to be exposed to death for Jesus' sake.*

357

28. *Then there passed by Midianite merchantmen; and they drew and lifted Joseph up out of the pit, and sold Joseph to the Ishmaelites for twenty pieces of silver: and they brought Joseph into Egypt.*

Joseph is sold even by his liberator. From a free man he becomes a slave. He was free in the sweet and peaceful love of God in which he lived; now he is sold as a slave. And to whom is he sold? To sin. Sold to sin! Oh, what a change! He is sold to sin, so that sin may exercise its tyranny over him; but he is not on that account rendered subject to sin. The state of *being sold* to sin and of being made its slave is very different from that of subjection to sin. St. Paul explains it of himself: *I am*, says he, *sold to sin;* and then he says that he is in *bondage under the law of sin which is in his members*. This is the distinction he makes between these two states.

29. *And Reuben returned to the pit, and not finding the child,*
30. *He rent his clothes, and came and said to his brethren, The child is no more, and what will become of me?*

There is always found some soul of too natural a tendency who would draw us from the conduct of providence : they would desire it seems, out of charity, to *draw* us *from the pit*—that is to say, from the cross, from *abandon*, from the loss by which God conducts us ; but God by His providence knows so well how to act His part, that none can draw us out of His hands.

31. *After that they took Joseph's coat and dipped it in the blood of a goat which they had killed.*
32. *And they sent it to his father.*
33. *And he recognised it and said: It is my son's coat, a cruel beast hath eaten him.*

Those who strip us in the order of Providence, of gifts and sensible graces, *dip* them *in blood ;* for all these sweetnesses and benefits of God are changed into apparent cruelty ; but it is a cruelty only superficial, and having nothing real but the figure. Everything becomes blood and carnage for such a soul : everything is a cross to it, but outwardly only ; for within, it is in peace through *abandon*.

Spiritual persons, hearing what is told of the apparent disaster of these souls, believe them lost, and say like Jacob, "These poor interior ones have been deceived, the *cruel beast has devoured them.*" Credulity finds a place even in the holiest souls, who, adding faith to calumny, believe at first that the *Demon* has *devoured* these simple persons, having caused them to fall into his illusions.

> 34. *Jacob rent his clothes, and covered himself with sackcloth, and wept for his son many days.*
>
> 36. *Meanwhile the Midianites sold Joseph in Egypt to Potiphar, an officer of Pharaoh's, and captain of his guard.*

These holy ones are afflicted, *weep*, and *do penance* for these abandoned persons, so as to entreat God's mercy. Jacob had not wept for Rachel, who was so dear to him, and he is so greatly afflicted for Joseph. The reason is, that regarding things in God, Rachel's death was useful and necessary, and he saw in that only the death of a truly lovely form, but which he desired only in God's will; whereas he is here surveying the disaster of a spiritual soul believed to be lost under the dominion of the Demon, although really it is holier than ever. Jacob saw only the tragic and bloody exterior, and he knew not that his son was full of life and repose.

Joseph is again *sold* a second time. Does it not seem as if he were born only for slavery and the cross? But as a noble soul finds its liberty in the fetters, so a soul abandoned to God is never freer than when it appears more a slave.

CHAPTER XXXIX.

> 1. *And Joseph was brought down to Egypt; and Potiphar, an officer of Pharaoh, captain of the guard, an Egyptian, bought him from the Ishmaelites, which had brought him down thither.*
>
> 2. *And the Lord was with Joseph, and he was a prosperous man.*

Is it not a conduct worthy of God's right hand to preserve so great souls under an exterior so lowly and reviled? *God was always with Joseph,* as He never leaves these dear abandoned ones, and they are never better than when they are most despaired of by every one; for it is then that God exercises a particular protection over them, which they experience so sensibly, that they cry out of the depth of bitterness with the prophet-king : *The Lord is my light and my salvation,* whom could I fear?

   3. *His master saw that the Lord was with him, and that He blessed him in all his actions.*

God mortifies and vivifies, and he sustains by the very hand that he strikes with. He gives mortal wounds ; but he puts the balm at the arrow's point, so that we cannot tell which is the most sensible—the grief, or the pleasure. It is a pleasure full of grief ; it is a grief full of pleasure. Oh God, dost thou not always kill thus !

   6. *Now Joseph was of a fair countenance, and very agreeable.*

   7. *And a long time afterwards his mistress cast her eyes upon him, and said to him, Sleep with me.*

   8. *But Joseph looked upon this crime with horror, and answered her,*

   9. *How can I commit so criminal an act, and sin against my God?*

Thou hast, oh Lord, redoubled blows, in which thou minglest much bitterness ! There are times that Thou probest and poisonest the wound. Oh why dost Thou not kill entirely? Might we not dare to call Thee cruel, since Thou preservest life only to have the pleasure of killing once again? But who could complain of Thee, save those that do not know Thee ? Thou appearest lovely to those very ones who experience only Thy severities, no longer feeling the sweetness of Thy love.

   12. *His mistress took him by his cloak, and said to him, Sleep with me? Then Joseph left his cloak in her hands, and fled, and got out of the house.*

Here is the grievous blow : he must perish, or sin. It seems, O God, that thou hast only given a little respite to Joseph with Potiphar in order to prepare him for harder blows.

Chapter XXXIX.

These are Thy master-strokes. Joseph is subjected to sin ; but, nevertheless, he triumphs over sin. These are thy salutarily-poisoned arrows, which mortally wound without killing. This is a calamity to be avoided *by flight.* Yes, Joseph, thou wilt avoid the reality of sin, and not the appearance ; for thou wilt pass for a sinner.

13. *And when this woman saw his garment in her hands, and that she had been despised,*

14. *She called the people of her house, and said to them, They have brought in this Hebrew slave to mock us. He wished to force me, and when I cried out,*

15. *He has left his cloak with me, and has fled.*

Thou must pass for a criminal although thou art innocent. Thou wilt be accused of the crime thou hast not committed, and thou wilt be looked upon as guilty by all. Thou wilt even be punished for it. This is a degree through which God makes many souls pass ; and this advances and finishes their death, because the exterior cross joined to the interior, the pain of destitution, of abandonment, of the confusion they bear, consummates all the sooner their mystic death. There are others in whom the crosses being great and heavy, both inwardly and outwardly, God is content with that, particularly if these persons are not destined for the conducting of others.

19. *And his master, too ready to believe the accusations of his wife, was greatly enraged.*

20. *And he caused Joseph to be put into the prison, where the King's prisoners were kept, and he was shut up.*

It does not end here for Joseph. Those even whom he has obliged the most must believe in the calumny ; he must pass several years in prison abandoned by all, and held as guilty. But oh, Joseph, thou art a prisoner and innocent : thou hast lost nothing of thine integrity : thou art happier an innocent prisoner than David a guilty king. Oh what a beautiful parallel might be drawn between these two persons, so that God's conduct over abandoned souls might be observed ! He will cause it to be done at the time He pleaseth. Some remain innocent and are punished as guilty ; others with the punishment have also the sin. Joseph becomes more a slave in proportion as he is more innocent. David yet continues to reign, although afflicted, punished, and guilty.

21. *But the Lord was with Joseph, and showed him mercy, and gave him favour in the sight of the keeper of the prison.*

22. *And the keeper of the prison committed to him the care of all the prisoners; there was nothing done there but by his order, the keeper entrusted to him everything,*

23. *And looked not to anything whatsoever under his hand, for the Lord was with Joseph, and made him prosper in all things.*

God's goodness is signalized in mingling the greatest bitternesses with sensible sweetnesses. So long as our Lord does not abandon the soul, and it is assured of His aid and presence, there is nothing so severe but becomes sweet; but when He conceals Himself, and we lose this so sweet a Presence, which consoles in all afflictions, oh, it is then that grief is extreme.

The innocent soul rules over all the world, and is never sub ject to it. Joseph, a prisoner and in chains, becomes the governor of the other prisoners. This is how these faithful servants of Jesus Christ in the midst even of their afflictions, continue to aid others; and when they are more afflicted in their ways, they would introduce every one to them, and make them walk therein. It is the effect of the truth contained in this way, to have a complete certainty of it for others, although we may have no assurance of it for ourselves.

CHAPTER XL.

1—5. *Two officers of the King of Egypt, his chief butler, and his chief baker being in prison, had each a dream on the same night, the interpretation of which was to be different.*

8. *They said afterwards to Joseph, We have had a dream, and we have no one to explain it to us. Joseph answered them, And who is the interpreter of dreams? Is it not God? Tell me what ye have dreamed.*

Chapter XL.

God, for the sake of these persons so fully abandoned to the conduct of His providence, often gives to sinners some extraordinary light so as to lead them to communicate it, and that thus they may be instructed of the ways He takes with souls, and that these poor wandering ones may come out of the captivity of sin. Joseph's reply is truly worthy of a faithful abandoned one, who, attributing nothing to himself, refers everything to God. This is what gives us a holy boldness, and leads us to undertake everything, leaning upon the Divine strength, from which we derive our origin, as Joseph derived it from Israel; nevertheless, little advanced souls attribute this often to pride and rashness.

> 12. *This is the interpretation of thy dream: The three branches are three days.*
>
> 13. *After which Pharaoh will remember the service thou hast rendered to him, and will restore thee to thy former charge.*
>
> 14. *—I pray thee only to remember me when this happiness shall come to thee.*
>
> 18. *He said also to the other, This is the interpretation of thy dream: The three baskets signify that thou hast but three days yet to live.*
>
> 19. *After which the King shall cause thy head to be cut off.*

The same word of God is often a word of life and a word of death; it renders liberty to some, drawing them out of the slavery of sin; and it innocently causes death to others afterwards from the bad use they make of it. It was not Joseph's word that caused the death of the baker, since the cause of it lay in the sin of him who had committed it—it warned him only that his death was nigh; but he took no measure to avoid it. We can escape sin by our own cares, sustained by God's grace and by penitence; but life comes from God alone: therefore Joseph prayed the butler when he would be re-established in favour *to remember him,* and the word of God he had announced to him, which very often the propriety causes to be forgot. The word of God is a seed, but hidden, however, in the ground, and bearing fruit in its own time.

> 21. *Pharaoh restored the chief butler to his place again, and he continued to give the cup to Pharaoh.*

22. *And he hanged the other, which verified the interpretation, which Joseph gave of their dreams.*

23. *Nevertheless the chief butler, when he found himself restored to favour, thought no more of his interpreter.*

God here brings to view His faithfulness in sustaining His word, which he has put into the mouth of His servants; and although its execution be delayed for some days, it is nevertheless found always true. But when one is in prosperity, one easily *forgets* him from whom the word has proceeded, unless God by a particular providence brings him to our remembrance. God also is pleased to permit this forgetfulness so as to augment the merit of His servants, by prolonging their sufferings; and to exercise so much the more their faith and their *abandon*, the more He seems to forget them.

CHAPTER XLI.

1. *Two years afterwards Pharaoh had a dream.*

9. *Then the chief butler remembered Joseph, and said to the king: I confess my sin.*

10. *Being in prison with the chief baker,*

12. *We had both a dream on the same night:*

13. *And a young man, an Hebrew, who was in the same prison,*

14. *Told us all that has since happened.*

Awaking and *remembering* God are admirable means to draw a soul out of prison, out of captivity and the shadow of death. After having had some hope of issuing out of its poor and destitute state, it passes yet several years in a total destitution and in an entire oblivion. There no longer even remains to it any hope, and it thinks only of remaining thus, like the eternal dead, who are thought of no more; it endeavours only to bear this state with *abandon*, and to be contented with it, seeing itself in the will of God, but it does not think ever to come out of it.

14. *Joseph was immediately brought out of the prison by the*

command of the king; and they shaved him, and made him change his raiment, and presented him before the king.

When it is buried in this manner in the oblivion of death, it is all astonished to see its *prison* opened, to see itself approached and stripped of this state of death, the marks of slavery taken from it by degrees, and itself *covered with the robe* of life and liberty. For sometimes this soul is as half asleep; it does not know whether it sleeps or wakes, whether it is a dream or reality, when suddenly it sees itself *drawn out of this obscure and gloomy place*, and placed in the open day of the true light. Then it knows the truth of its change, and so much the more as it is brought to *appear before the King*. It is then from this moment placed in the resuscitated life, but it is not yet established in the resuscitated state, which has many other advantages. God makes use of this very word, which had been hid in the earth of forgetfulness, to draw this soul out of death and eternal oblivion, as the Son of God by His word drew Lazarus from the tomb.

15. *And Pharaoh said unto Joseph: I have dreamed a dream, and there is none that can interpret it. I have heard it said that thou hadst a singular gift of interpreting them.*

16. *And Joseph answered him, and said: It will be God and not I who will give a favourable interpretation to the king.*

There was no person in all Egypt *who could interpret* Pharoah's dreams; for what passes in the heart of God is only known by the Spirit of God. Joseph's reply shows that it is only self-renunciation and the loss of all desire to be anything which leads such a soul to attribute nothing to itself. On the contrary, persuaded that it is but a feeble instrument, and that God can do everything without it, it declares itself with a frankness worthy of so high a truth. *God*, without it, can perform all that He does by it; and if He uses it, all the glory must be rendered to Him. Therefore, it leads the creature, beforehand, to render all the glory of it to God, and to regard no good done out of Him.

17. *Pharaoh then related to him what he had seen. It seemed to me, he said, that I stood upon the bank of a river,*

18. *From whence came up seven fat-fleshed and well-favoured kine, and they fed in the meadows.*

This *bank of the river* represents the waters either of Baptism or penitence, out of which a soul comes forth very beautiful, and in a most perfect fatness. *The seven kine* or the *seven years* which they signify, are the usual time that souls remain in the acquisition of virtues. They appear then all *beautiful*, and no defect is seen in them, because God gives them so many graces that they are as in a most abundant *pasture*, where they become strong, fat, beautiful, and very agreeable.

19. *Afterwards there came up seven others, so horrible and so lean that I have never seen their like in Egypt.*

20. *And these latter devoured and swallowed up the first.*

Those years, so agreeable and so sweet, and so well watered with calm and tranquil waters, having passed, the soul is much astonished, when thinking on nothing less, to see them *devoured* by these other *years* that follow them, but of so great sterility and famine, that without the provisions that had been made, death from hunger must occur. It must be observed that Scripture does not say that *the lean kine* killed the fat, but that they *devoured them*, which shows that, in this time of so strange an avidity, all the graces and virtues of the other years are contained therein, although nothing of them may appear outwardly, just as the fat kine were contained within the lean, although nothing of them appeared without.

21. *They appeared in no wise filled with them, but, on the contrary, they were as lean and frightsome as at first.*

These *lean* kine continue to be *as hideous* and disfigured after devouring the fat ones as they were before. Oh, this is the mystery hidden from men not divinely enlightened, and revealed to the little ones; it is even hid from those in whom it takes place. There appears outwardly only ugliness and deformity, and all the beauty of the king's daughter is hidden within her during these seven years. There appear only defects on all sides; everything seems to be void of grace, as these kine are of flesh. Nevertheless, it is certain that there never was more of it; but it remains hidden in the frightful belly of dryness until the day of manifestation. The beauty of the first years make the others appear *so ugly* that *Pharaoh*, who represents the world, *avers that he had never seen their like in all his kingdom.*

25. *Joseph answered: God has made known unto Pharaoh what He is about to do.*

26. *The seven good kine signify seven years of abundance which will come.*

27. *The seven ill-favoured kine mark the seven years of famine that are to follow them.*

30. *The famine will be so great that it will cause all the abundance which preceded it to be forgotten.*

The souls of grace soon judge of what comes from God by the experience they have of it. Thus *Joseph* immediately *assures* the King that his dream is divine. It is the property of the time of *abundance* to take away all thought of the *famine* and *sterility* that is to follow it, and it is also usual for persons in their trials to forget all the good they had possessed. Nothing of it remains to them any more, because God so effaces all trace of it outwardly that it seems as if it had been only a deception, and they had never really belonged to God. Nevertheless, they were never more His. Confessors even doubt them. It is only such an experience and light as Joseph's that can discover the mystery; for this famine must consume all the earth, and nothing remain, so that the great want may destroy the great abundance; for if there remained anything this would not be entire loss, and this mystery would not be accomplished. Thou must then, Oh soul, expect to lose, without reserve, all that thou possessest, and thou must measure the greatness of thy loss by the greatness of thy possession. The more thou hast been beautiful and agreeable, and the object of the admiration of peoples, the more thou must become ugly, deformed, and the object of their horror and contempt. Oh, conduct of my God! To make the soul return to its origin it must lose all Thy gifts. Thou grantest them to it to make it come out of sin and to make it return into its heart, from which it had strayed, and Thou takest them away from it to make it come out from this same heart and to lose it into Thee. Thy gifts drive away sin, and fill the soul with Thy graces, and Thou drivest Thy gifts from it to fill it with Thyself! Oh, truth too unknown!

33. *Now therefore let Pharaoh look out a man discreet and wise, and set him over the land of Egypt.*

34. *And let him appoint officers in all the provinces, who during the seven years of plenty that are to come may gather into the public granaries the fifth part of the fruits of the earth.*

The enlightened director, foreseeing what must happen, obliges the soul to lay up as much provisions as it can, for the more that it profits by the first graces, given to it in abundance, it will be the better for it. I confess that its loss will also be all the greater; but although it lose everything belonging to itself, yet all is found again in God, preserved in His sacred *storehouses.* Therefore, it is a matter of consequence to choose a skilful and experienced director, to whom we may trust the conducting of everything.

37. *This counsel pleased Pharaoh and all his ministers.*

38. *And he said to them: Where can we find a man so full of the Spirit of God as this?*

39. *He said then to Joseph: Since God hath shown thee all that thou hast told us, how can we find one wiser than thou, or like to thee?*

In the choice of a director we must always prefer him who has most of *the Spirit of God.* Pharaoh gives us an example of it. Far from laughing, as some do, at the advice given them for their good, and of which they never profit, he took for conductor, in an affair of this importance, the very one who had given him *this counsel,* and caused everything he commanded to be punctually followed out.

41. *And Pharaoh said unto Joseph: See, I have set thee over all the land of Egypt.*

42. *And Pharaoh took off his ring from his hand and put it upon Joseph's hand, and arrayed him in vestures of fine linen, and put a gold chain about his neck.*

The power which the king gives him *over all Egypt* marks the authority of direction. Now Joseph is established and confirmed in the state of Resurrection. Not only is freedom given to him, but he receives it with many other advantages which he had not before his captivity whilst he was with his father. God restores to the resuscitated and renewed soul all the graces He had rendered to it before its disaster, and there is added to them an infinity of others which it never would have thought it ought to hope for.

> 43. *And he made him ride in the second chariot which he had; and they cried before him, Bow the knee; and he made him ruler over all the land of Egypt.*

Who would have told Joseph two years before, when he thought only to finish his days in an obscure prison, that he was to be *governor of all Egypt?* Who would have told this abandoned soul, destitute, and covered with darkness and the shadow of death, that so great an evil was to produce so great a good? It could not have believed it; yet it has been found most real.

> 45. *He also changed his name, and called him in the Egyptian language, The Saviour of the World. And he gave him to wife Asenath, daughter of Potiphera, priest of On.*

Behold then the resuscitated soul! see it confirmed in its resurrection, and loaded with graces. It is then that it arrives at the purity of its origin; it is then also that *the new name* is given to it, as to all the fathers: Thou shalt be no more called Joseph, but *the Saviour of Egypt.* It is always after the resurrection, and when the soul has arrived at its origin, that the new name is given to it, that is to say, that the perfect renewal is made; and it is then that there is celebrated the marriage of the Lamb.

> 45. *And Joseph went out over all the land of Egypt.*
> 46. *And Joseph was thirty years old when he stood before Pharaoh, King of Egypt.*
> 50. *Before the famine came, Joseph had two children by his wife Asenath.*
> 51. *And Joseph called the name of the first-born Manasseh: for God, said he, hath made me forget all my toil, and all my father's house.*

It is also always at this time that the Apostolic life commences when we do not begin it of ourselves, but when we enter into it only by the command of God; which is so well figured in *Joseph* after this renewal *making the tour of all* the provinces of *Egypt.* We must be renewed before operating. Jesus Christ, our Divine model, passed thirty years in his hidden life before appearing in public; and he did so only after experiencing the temptation in the desert. This relation of the ancient figures to their divine truth will enrapture all who penetrate it.

From the time of this renewal we begin to beget *children* to Jesus Christ. Joseph here *forgets all past labours,* as in poverty he forgot all the graces he had received. This is the property of each of these states.

> 52. *He called the name of the second, Ephraim, saying, God has made me fruitful in the land of my poverty.*

Joseph, well instructed in interior ways, acknowledges that all his blessings have come to him from his poverty ; because it is in the time that the seed remains hid in the ground that it rots, sprouts, and bears much fruit.

CHAPTER XLII.

> 21. *Joseph's brethren said one to another, It is rightly that we suffer this, for we have sinned against our brother—— Therefore does God afflict us thus.*
>
> 22. *And Reuben answered them, saying, Spake I not unto you saying, do not sin against the child; and ye would not hear? Therefore, behold, also his blood is required.*

God always makes the wicked feel sooner or later the punishment merited by the persecution they cause to the good; and that also is useful to them, because it makes them return into themselves.

> 23. *And they knew not that Joseph understood them, for he spake unto them by an interpreter.*
>
> 24. *But as he could no longer restrain his tears, he turned himself about a little, and wept.*

Chapter XLIII.

The goodness of a heart that is God's cannot be enough admired: he could not see his greatest persecutors suffer the least thing without being afflicted at it, more than they are themselves.

CHAPTER XLIII.

8. *Judah said unto his father:*

9. *I will be surety for the child; of my hand shalt thou require him. If I bring him not unto thee, and set him before thee, then let me bear the blame for ever.*

So long as it is only Reuben who asks Benjamin from Jacob he is not willing to give him, because he was not inclined to trust him to the conduct of men; but as soon as God explains Himself by the mouth of *Judah*, who is the one He has chosen to be the father of His Son, then Jacob gives him without difficulty, abandoning him thus to the conduct of Providence. The children of men act quite differently. They blindly trust themselves to other men—to a lawyer, to a doctor, to a friend, to a coachman—and they believe they would lose themselves if they fully trusted God.

32. *They served Joseph apart, and his brethren by themselves; and the Egyptians that did eat with him by themselves; for it is not permitted the Egyptians to eat with the Hebrews, for that is an abomination to the Egyptians.*

The saints, full of the Spirit of God, have admirable consideration not to offend men in what is immaterial. *Joseph* finds the means not to repel the *Egyptians*, and yet to regale his brethren in his company and in their presence, causing them all to be *served apart* on different tables, although in the same place; and thus, honouring both, he had the consolation of eating with his brethren and with the Egyptian lords, and, what is more, of entering in that into the will of God; but all that was not without mystery. Joseph's brethren were not of an interior elevation equal to his own to sit at table with him; he sends them only meats that had been served before him, so that they might have part in the fulness of his grace and in the unction of his spirit; and the best part fell to *Benjamin*, who was the most united to him, as well by spirit as by blood.

CHAPTER XLIV.

18. *Judah said to Joseph,*

32. *Rather let me be thy slave, since I became surety for the lad, saying unto my father, If I bring him not back unto thee, let me bear the blame for ever.*

34. *For I cannot return unto my father unless the lad be with us.*

This courage of *Judah* in giving himself up for his brother already marks beforehand that He who should give Himself up for all men would be born of him, and thus giving himself as a hostage for a single man he was the figure of Him who was to become the ransom for all. What does it also express to us by his not wishing to *return to his father except the child be with him*, if not that Christ, of the tribe of Judah, desires not to re-ascend unto His Father until He conduct there with Him the human nature freed from its captivity, and His dear people whom He will have redeemed?

CHAPTER XLV.

4. *Joseph spake gently unto his brethren, and said to them, I am your brother whom you sold into Egypt.*

5. *Fear not, neither grieve ye for having sold me into this land, for God has sent me before you into Egypt to preserve your life.*

A soul of this degree never attributes to its persecutors the persecutions that have been made against it, but, seeing everything in God as an admirable order of providence, it turns all to *God.* Joseph was most faithful in acting thus. This is what makes us love our enemies as much as our friends, for we never stop to look on the evil they do, but on the good that results from it. In this sense the commandment given us by Jesus Christ to love our enemies is found so easy by those penetrated with a lively faith, who have the taste of His love, that we could not help doing it even though He should not have commanded it.

> 8. *It was not by your design that I have been sent hither, but by the will of God, who hath made me as a father to Pharaoh, the lord of all his house, and the prince of the whole of Egypt.*

Joseph, however, confesses that that was not the *design* of his brethren when they persecuted him, but the will *of God*, who causes everything to be conducted according to His eternal design.

He gives them, moreover, to know something of *God's designs* over him, and of His impenetrable conduct of the chosen, whom He humbles only to raise again; and also of the truth of his dreams, of which they saw the fulfilment.

> 13. *Tell my father of the greatness of my glory, and all that ye have seen in Egypt; haste ye and bring him to me.*

Joseph does not say this out of ostentation, but because he knows that his father is acquainted with the secrets of the mystic life; and he gives him proofs of his state by the favours he distributes to all, and by the gifts he makes to him.

> 23. *He sent silver and raiment for his father, with ten asses laden with all the riches of Egypt.*

These *ten asses* laden with *all the riches of Egypt*, are, as I have already said previously (ch. 24 v. 10), the ten commandments of God; but enriched and set off by an admirable practice, performed in God Himself, and known only to the most advanced interior persons.

> 24. *He also sent away his brethren; and when they were setting out he said to them, See that ye fall not out by the way.*

This counsel of charity is so necessary to all, that really it is only union with the neighbour joined to trust in God, that prevents ennui and chagrin in so long a journey as that of the interior, and that makes everything succeed happily.

26. *And when Jacob heard that his son Joseph was alive, and that he ruled throughout all the land of Egypt, he started as from a profound sleep, and could not believe it.*

Although Jacob was instructed by his experience of the mystic way, of its reverses, and of the successes by which God vivifies after having mortified; yet he believed he was dreaming, so much was he surprised at so strange a conduct. It is in vain for us to be warned of the surprising routes through which God causes souls to pass: when we see their effects, we yet continue to be in astonishment and distrust.

27. *But when he saw the chariots which Joseph his son sent to him, his spirit revived.*

28. *And Israel said, It is enough; Joseph my son is yet alive: I will go and see him before I die.*

But seeing the fruits of the state, they can no longer doubt, and they must say: Assuredly, this soul *lives* in God; and *that is sufficient.*

CHAPTER XLVI.

3. *God said to Jacob, I am the Almighty, the God of thy father. Fear not, but go into Egypt, for I will make thee the chief of a great people in that land.*

As Jacob had hesitated at so strange an occurrence, God reassures him, putting him in mind of *His omnipotence.* He declares to him that this is one of His master-strokes; and that being the *God of his father,* whom He delivered from the knife that was raised to slay him, it is He Himself who enjoins him to *go into Egypt.*

I am the Almighty, the God of thy father. These words are so expressive to make known God's power and faithfulness in what He does on behalf of the abandoned souls, that I cannot help repeating them. Who will fear to abandon himself into His hands, since He calls Himself *the Almighty God* of these souls who are abandoned to Him without reserve? Is not everything secure for them, although in the midst of the greatest despair?

4. *I will go with thee, and will bring thee back also when thou returnest, and Joseph will close thine eyes.*

This promise was not only for Jacob; but also for all those who, like him, would fully abandon themselves even *to go into Egypt* for the love of God; that is to say to quit the region of peace, and go by the will of God into the land of trouble and corruption, according as it is necessary and as God requires it. It is so clear that God spoke in the person of Jacob to the abandoned souls, true children of Israel, and not to him personally, since at the same time that He promises to bring *him back from Egypt*, He assures him that he will die there, predicting that Joseph *will shut his eyes.* God, after making the souls that are abandoned to Him go into the Egypt of trial and temptation, never fails to *reconduct* them into their region of repose.

29. *When Jacob had arrived, Joseph mounted his chariot, and went to meet his father, and he fell on his neck, and embraced him, and wept.*

It would not have been a complete resurrection for *Joseph* if God had not restored *his father* to him, that is to say, if He had not conducted him into his origin: and this is what happens, as I have said, after the resurrection, when the soul finds itself reunited to God its origin, with the purity in which it had issued from Him.

CHAPTER XLVIII.

14. *And Israel stretched out his right hand, and laid it upon Ephraim's head, who was the younger, and his left hand upon Manasseh's head, guiding his hands wittingly; for Manasseh was the first born.*

17. *And Joseph held up his father's hand, to remove it from Ephraim's head unto Manasseh's head.*

18. *And Joseph said unto his father, Not so, my father; for this is the first born; put thy right hand upon his head.*

This *change of hands* which Israel made was not without 'stery: he gave the birthright to the younger; because the ərer we approach God, the more ought we to become child-ı; and the greater we are in ourselves and before men, the s are we before God. Therefore Jacob, by the spirit of ᵒphecy, affirmed that the little one would be preferred to the ᵗat: which Jesus Christ has so often declared himself.

19. *But Jacob refused, saying, I know it, my son, I know it well. He also shall be a chief of great peoples, and his seed shall be multiplied; but his brother, who is younger than he, shall be greater than he.*

ʔ1. *And Israel said unto Joseph, Behold I die: but God shall be with you, and bring you again unto the land of your fathers.*

ʔ2. *Moreover, I have given to thee one portion above thy brethren.*

Ӷhis repetition of Jacob's: *I know it, my son, I know it well,* ws with what understanding he did that, assuring that the .nt people, that is to say, living in the simple state, would ᵒme very much *greater than the other.* Jacob again assures eph of the confirmation of his state in which he is estab-ed, promising him that *God* will be always *with him;* which ᵗks the confirmation in grace : and because of the persecu-ıs and sufferings he had borne, *he gives him a portion of his ᵗs above his brethren,* signifying by that how much God pre-ed him to the others.

CHAPTER XLIX.

And Jacob called unto his sons, and said, Gather your-selves together. that I may tell you that which shall befal you in the last days.

Chapter XLIX.

Jacob announces to his sons what was to happen touching the interior kingdom and coming of Jesus Christ.

4. *Reuben, unstable as water, thou shalt not excel:*

8. *Judah, thy brethren shall praise thee; thy hand shall put thine enemies under the yoke; thy father's children shall worship thee.*

He had said to Reuben, that all the *strength* coming of man, *would flow away like water;* but for *Judah,* in whom there was contained Jesus Christ, chief of all the true interior souls, he assures him that *his brethren,* the devout and not mystical souls, *will praise him;* that he *will triumph over his enemies* in Jesus Christ, who has destroyed all. For the truly mystical souls have no power of their own; all their strength is in God alone. This expression, *the sons of thy father,* by which he seems to distinguish them from his brethren, marks that he means to speak of the souls entirely abandoned to the supreme will of God, who are the true children of Israel who will worship God with a worship worthy of him; for it is only these worshippers who worship in spirit and in truth.

9. *Judah is a young lion. Thou art risen, my son, to carry off the prey. In reposing thou art couched like a lion and a lioness. Who will rouse him?*

This word *lion* shows his strength; but he calls him a *little lion,* to show that his strength is in his Father and in his nature: his Father is his son, and his son is his Father. This is the Lion that none can conquer.

Thou art indeed *risen to carry off thy prey,* since thou containest in thyself nothing less than the blood of a God by whom the whole world—earth and heaven—is to be conquered.

But to show that he speaks of interior souls, who carry off the prey because they remain victorious on every point, he explains it thus: My son, *in reposing* in the mystic sleep, *thou art couched* in God *like the lion and the lioness,* who fear nothing, because of their boldness and their strength: for the lion rests secure in his strength; and this soul reposes safely in God, who is its strength. Therefore he adds, *Who will rouse him up?* Meaning, who would have the courage to come where this soul is? Could all hell *trouble the repose* of a soul that is permanently in God?

Genesis.

This couching can be also understood of the repose of the Word incarnated in the womb of Mary, for he was couched within her chaste form as the lion in his cavern.

> 10. *The Sceptre shall not be taken away from Judah, nor the Prince from his race, until he that is to be sent is come; and it is he that will be the expectation of all nations.*

The sceptre shall always remain in his house, because he is master of all the world in this state, his kingdom being God alone: by the state of union and simplicity, he possesses a kingdom within himself through the interior peace, which renders him master of his passions. But when *He that is to be sent shall come*, which is done by the mystic incarnation, in which the Word is given in the state of transformation, then this kingdom will be taken away, for this soul no longer possessing itself, Jesus possesses all within it; and all possessions of its own and all kingdoms are reunited in Him. Thus is He the *expectation of the nations*, and of the souls called to participate in this happiness.

> 11. *He shall wash his garments in wine, and his clothes in the blood of grapes.*

This wine is no other than the blood of Jesus Christ; for these souls have no longer any purity proper to them, nor merit peculiar to themselves; but they have everything in Jesus Christ: thus do they expect nothing of themselves, nor by any effort on their part: but with whatever misery they may be covered, everything is found cleansed in the blood of the grape Jesus Christ, who has been under the wine press, and who has given Himself to His friends as the wine. There is nothing, then, to be feared any more for these souls made white in the blood of the Lamb.

> 12. *His eyes are more beautiful than wine, and his teeth whiter than milk.*

His eyes more beautiful than wine, signifies the power of His charity, looking upon the wretchedness of men to succour them. They denote also the knowledge joined to charity, being lost in the Divine love. The purity of His actions, represented by *the teeth*, surpasses all that can be said of them, for they are done in innocence.

> 22. *Joseph is the fruitful son; he will be multiplied more and more. His countenance is beautiful and agreeable.*
>
> 24. *He has placed his bow in strength, and the chains of his hands and arms have been broken by the hand of the Almighty God of Jacob. From thence is gone out the shepherd and the stone of Israel.*

The abandoned soul dwells in its strength although surrounded by feebleness; because it *has placed* all the *bow* of its strength *in the Almighty*, who is its God. But after the years of its trials and captivity are passed, the hands of God, who is *the Almighty One* of Jacob, *loose its arms and hands*, and render them fit for great things.

From thence is gone out the shepherd of Israel. This can be understood in two ways; first, that his hands being loosed, the shepherd issues from this deliverance: for it is after the soul has been set at liberty by the resurrection and renewal that it is fit to conduct others. The other, that from the Mighty One of Jacob, who is God, is gone out the conductor of the interior people, Jesus Christ, the true shepherd.

By *the stone of Israel* is meant the foundation. This foundation is also Jesus Christ, foundation-stone of the spiritual edifice, which has only worth and stability because founded upon Jesus Christ, firm stone and living rock, and not upon the sand of self-inventions: another explanation is, that Israel being the father of souls abandoned to God, all this race is founded upon him as upon the stone.

> 25. *The God of thy father will help thee; and the Almighty will load thee with blessings of the Heaven above, with blessings of the deep that lieth under, with blessings of the breasts, and of the womb.*

The God of thy father, the God of Israel and of the true abandoned ones, and *the Almighty*, He to whom nothing is difficult, *will load thee with blessings from Heaven above:* meaning, that they will not only have the graces and favours of heaven given in the state of passivity of light and love, where everything comes assuredly from on high, the certitude being

ven with it; but they will also have *the blessing of the deep
nderneath*, that is to say, temptations and distresses, which are
ie appendages of the abyss. This is understood also of the
terior hell through which such chosen souls as these pass (at
ast some), and which, with all its consequences and infernal
ipours (which have nothing but what is horrible), yet con-
nues to be, for those who know how to make the use of it that
od designs, *a blessing* as much and even greater than the first.

The last *blessing* is distinguished into two kinds; the one of
e breasts, the milk of which represents the facility of aiding
iritual children in this way, and nourishing them with this
iritual milk of contemplation; the other *of the womb*, by which
meant the production of these same children in Jesus Christ.
or the grace of spiritual generation is different from that of
urishment and education. The first begets in Jesus Christ,
it cannot nourish: the second nourishes, but does not beget:
it the two together form the perfection of the apostolic way:
erefore this so complete a blessing is reserved for Joseph, who
in that state.

26. *The blessings given thee by thy father are sustained by those
he has received from his fathers, until the desire of the
everlasting hills is come. Let these blessings be upon the
head of Joseph,—of him who is as a Nazarite amongst
his brethren.*

*The blessings given by Jacob to Joseph are sustained by those
hich Jacob has received from his fathers;* because they are
·tified by the faith and *abandon* from which he derives his
igin, and this is what must sustain his blessings. He certi-
s also by these words, that his ancestors have walked in the
ne way, and that they uphold so extraordinary a blessing by
e example of their life *until the desire* of these souls, who have
peared like mountains and *hills* by the eminence of their
liness, *be accomplished*, that is to say, be reduced into unity,
ien all desire is lost.

But the truest sense is, that the example of his ancestors
ist sustain abandoned souls in so strange a way, until Jesus
irist, *the desire* of the saints, *be come* to be their preacher and
idel; and until by the mystic incarnation wrought in the soul,
exists in Him alone without mediums, even the most holy.

This blessing *will be above Joseph's head;* because although

Chapter L

Joseph is very elevated in the mystic life, nevertheless Jesus Christ is infinitely more so; and there is nothing so elevated that is not below Him, since He is the beginning and end of every way.

CHAPTER L.

16. *Thy father before dying commanded us,*

17. *To make this petition to thee from him: I pray thee to forget the crime of thy brethren, and this heinous wickedness they have committed against thee. We pray thee also to pardon this iniquity of the servants of God thy Father.*

19. *And Joseph replied unto them: Fear not: can we resist the will of God?*

20. *Ye thought to do evil against me; but God has changed it into good, so as to elevate me as ye now see me, and to save many people.*

These Hebrew brethren feared vengeance, for they knew not the generosity of persons in whom God reigns alone, and how forgetful they are of the injuries done unto them. This is what leads them to take the title of *the servants of God the Father of Joseph,* so as to engage him to pardon them, well knowing that nothing was more efficacious with so holy a man as to bring God to his remembrance, above all under this amiable quality of father.

But Joseph, established in the state of the Will of God, which is the highest perfection, speaks to them as a man well instructed in his ways, and says to them, that everything has taken place *in the Will of God,* which none can resist. He adds: *Fear not: can we resist this Divine Will,* which conducts everything infallibly, and which even makes use of the evil wills of men to attain its end, which changes evil into good, and elevates the soul by that which was intended to abase it? Sin even, whose nature is so hurtful to us, in the hand of God becomes useful to us; because He makes everything turn into good.

Oh Divine Will, from which everything derives its origin, and in whom everything terminates as in its end, how few souls Thou hast that are perfectly abandoned to all Thy commands!

THE DEEPER CHRISTIAN LIFE

ARE YOU INTERESTED IN READING ABOUT THE DEEPER CHRISTIAN LIFE?

If you are, let us suggest the order in which to read the following books, all of which have been written on the deepest aspescts of Christian Life.

By all means, begin with *The Divine Romance*. Then we recommend *Experiencing the Depths of Jesus Christ* and *Practicing His Presence*. Follow these with *Final Steps in Christian Maturity* and *The Inward Journey*.

For a study in brokenness, read *A Tale of Three Kings*, a favorite with thousands of believers all over the world.

To discover who you are in Jesus Christ, read *Turkeys and Eagles*, a masterfully told tale containing the very heart of the gospel as it pertains to living the Christian Life.

The books entitled *The Spiritual Guide, Jeanne Guyon Speaks Again* and *Fenelon's Letters*, all help to solidify, expand and buttress the things you will have read in the previous books.

You might also desire to read Guyon's studies of *Genesis, Exodus, Job, Song of Songs* and *Revelation*, thereby gaining her view of what she referred to as "The Scripture, seen from *the interior way*."

ARE YOU INTERESTED IN CHURCH LIFE?

Many Christians are interested in the vessel which is to contain the deeper Christian life . . . that is, the experience of church life.

We also recommend you read *Torch of the Testimony*, which recounts the awesome story of church life during the dark ages; and *Revolution* (vol. 1), which tells the story of the first twenty years of "church life" on the earth.

Our Mission, Letters To A Devastated Christian, and *Preventing A Church Split* were published specifically for Christians who have gone through - or are about to go through - the trauma of a church split . . . a devastating experience virtually every Christian will go through at least once. Because these three books (and *A Tale of Three Kings*) are practically the only books written on this subject, you may wish to share these books with a friend who might need them.

These books are available through your local Christian book store. The following prices are for the year of 1989 only. All books are paperback unless otherwise noted.

BOOKS BY GENE EDWARDS

BOOKS BY JEANNE GUYON

COMMENTARIES BY JEANNE GUYON

BOOKS BY OTHER AUTHORS

THE SEEDSOWERS
Christian Books Publishing House
P.O. Box 3368
Auburn, ME 04212-3368